No B1P
86/87

87/14

The Miraculous Birth
OF
LANGUAGE

The Miraculous Birth

OF

LANGUAGE

BY

RICHARD ALBERT WILSON

PROFESSOR OF ENGLISH LANGUAGE AND
LITERATURE IN THE UNIVERSITY OF SASKATCHEWAN

PREFACE BY

GEORGE BERNARD SHAW

PHILOSOPHICAL LIBRARY

NEW YORK

TO

MY WIFE

CONTENTS

7

8   *Contents*

Contents

PREFACE

By George Bernard Shaw

This book by Professor Wilson is one in which I should like everyone to be examined before being certified as educated or eligible for the franchise or for any scientific, religious, legal, or civil employment. My own profession is, technically, that of a master of language; and I have been plagued all my life by scientists, clergymen, politicians, and even lawyers, who talk like parrots, repeating words and phrases picked up from one another by ear without a moment's thought about their meaning, and accept mere association of ideas as an easy substitute for logic. They are often good fellows and even clever fellows; but they are not rational. And they are incurably addicted to their personal habits, which they call human nature.

The main controversy in my early days was about Evolution. It was started by Charles Darwin, a great naturalist, who upset both the Evolutionists and the Edenists (now calling themselves Fundamentalists) by bringing forward an array of instances in which the changes attributed to divinely purposed evolutionary developments could be accounted for by what he called Natural Selection: that is, by circumstances favoring the survival and multiplication of whatever natural varieties happened to be fittest to survive in the general struggle for subsistence. It was as if someone had shewn that the fact that most men's hats fit them, usually accounted for by the belief that they were made on purpose to fit them, could be accounted for on the hypothesis that hats occur in nature like wild strawberries, and that men picking them up discard those that do not fit and retain and wear those that do.

Such a suggestion would have been received, one would suppose, as a clever *jeu d'esprit,* to be taken seriously only to the extent of its calling attention to the fact that alongside evolutionary development has gone on the chapter of accidents and of changes forced on living creatures by the need to adapt themselves to external circumstances instead of obeying the evolutionary urge. Yet in the middle of the nineteenth century it produced an intellectual revolution in the biological, clerical, and philosophical professions generally. They had been compelled on pain of ostracism and financial ruin to work, write, and think on the assumption that the apologues in the book of Genesis are statements of scientific facts, and that the universe is the work of a grotesque tribal idol described in the book of Numbers as God, who resolves to destroy the human race, but is placated by a pleasant smell of roast meat brought to its nostrils by Noah. Any baptized and confirmed person questioning this assumption could be, and still can be, indicted for apostasy, and sentenced to penalties as severe as those reserved for manslaughter and treason. The intensity of the revolt against this limitation among scientists, philosophers, and thinkers of all sorts can hardly be imagined nowadays.

Unfortunately, when a reaction is produced by unbearable persecution, people do not sit down to a judicial examination of their beliefs so as to retain what is valid in them. Instead, they perform the operation known as emptying the baby out with the bath. They do not weed the garden: they tear up everything that grows in it, flower and fruit and vegetable as well as weed, and throw them all on the compost heap. Much as the scientists and philosophers (the best of them were the same people) hated the Fundamentalist's God, they had never been able to dispose satisfactorily of Paley's puzzle. If you find something as full of purpose and contrivance as a watch, he argued, you know that it did not make itself: somebody must have contrived it and made it. Napoleon pointed to the stars and asked "Who made all that?" The only reply was "Well, who made the maker?" Such logic chopping is not solid enough to stand against the mass of facts which seem contrived and designed. When Charles Darwin pointed out a host of instances in which a semblance of design had been produced by the chapter of accidents, the scientists embraced him as their deliverer. They threw over not only Noah's idol but all the other Scriptural attempts to personify or allegorize a creator as well.

They went further—far beyond Darwin, who was never a Darwinian. They lost their tempers if anyone hinted that there was any purpose or design in the universe at all. They set up a creed called Determinism, compared to which the story of Noah was cheerful and encouraging. One of its tenets was a topsy-turvy view of Causation in which the cause was itself an effect, and could not help itself. Samuel Butler, a sheepfarmer turned painter and painter turned philosopher, perceiving that Darwin had "banished mind from the universe," made war on him with all the literary weapons at his command, which were considerable; but he was immediately ostracized as maliciously unscientific. Challenged to explain the difference between a live body and a dead one, the physiologists declared that there was no difference. Not only mind, but life of any sort, was banished from the universe; and Materialism went stark raving mad. The author of this book calls it Mechanistic; but the Materialists dislike the term; for a machine, like Paley's watch, is a product of purpose and design; and this the ultra-Darwinians would not tolerate at any price.

The man in the street did not care. To him Darwin was a crank accusing him of being a developed ape. The religious sects found Genesis and St. Paul more comforting than pessimistic godlessness. A human society which, very wicked and evil in many ways, was redeemable by a blood sacrifice, and, since it was managing to survive, must be led in the long run by its saints rather than by its sinners, could at least bear thinking of, especially when it was borne in mind that our human life was only a brief purgatorial prelude to an eternity of bliss. But a wicked, evil, cruelly disease-ridden world which was also entirely senseless was a horror beyond words.

No matter. The most unwholesome food is welcome to the starving; and the scientific world gorged itself with Natural Selection. For the Bible was smashed at last. The 39 articles were reduced to absurdity. People stopped going to church in all directions. Hell was abolished. Jehovah was exposed as an impostor whose real name was Jarvey. Science said so; and everything that Science said was true, and everything that the clergy said was false. Talk of emptying the baby out with the bath! Babies were emptied out by the dozen with the deluge. Herod's massacre of the innocents was a joke in comparison.

Of course this was great nonsense; but it occurred for all that among people who were mentally active enough to be capable of a revolution in thought. A handful of people like Butler and myself saw that Natural Selection, far from being, as the public supposed, a discovery of something new called Evolution, was in fact a repudiation and castration of Evolution, depriving it of its moral basis in faith, hope, and charity; but our view went beyond the comprehension of the public, and some of our conclusions seemed irreconcilable. Though we were as anti-Edenist and anti-Paul as the crudest atheists and agnostics, we were classed with them and at the same time repudiated by them. Rousseau had said to the Churches, "Get rid of your miracles and the whole world will fall at the feet of Christ"; but we insisted that the world was full of miracles: for instance, the resurrection of life every spring was a miracle so stupendous that the cures of lameness and blindness, and even the raising of Lazarus of which Rousseau was thinking, were mere conjuring tricks in comparison.

It was very puzzling. How could people who were "infidels" believe in miracles and go far beyond the Bible in wonders and visions and prophecies? Infidels were people who did not believe in anything: how then could they have the face to call for an oceanic credulity as to the vital possibilities of the future? They do not believe in God, these people; yet here is this man Shaw telling us that if God becomes convinced that Man is a political failure, incapable of solving the problems raised by his own powers of reproduction and aggregation, God will supersede him by a new species as surely as the dinosaurus was superseded by Tom, Dick and Harry, Jill, Jane and Kate. What do they mean by God? What do we mean by God? The 39 articles tell us that God has neither body, parts, nor passions, and that we must accept the Bible as His word, though it describes Him as having all three. We shall lose caste if we don't go to church; but we shall gain it if we buy a motor car and drive in the country in it on Sunday; and, after all, the Smiths and Joneses have bought cars and have not been to church since; and no one has cut them for it.

As a run in the country brings better sermons from Nature than most persons can preach, perhaps the cars did more good than harm; but the balance was not always on that side. When Ibsen shewed that our ideals were often poisonous, when the Socialists shewed that our morals and economics were out-of-date and stale, when the Evolutionists and ultra-Darwinists alike made it impossible for any instructed person to accept the books of Moses as the work of a competent astro-physicist, over went all the baths and out went all the babies. Vivisectors claimed that science acknowledged no morals; plutocrats held that business is business and nothing else; Anacreontic writers put vine leaves in their hair and drank or drugged themselves to death; sadists and flagellomaniacs outfaced the humanitarians in the criminal courts; bright young things daubed their cheeks with paint and their nails and lips with vermilion, made love to soldiers, kept up their spirits with veronal tablets, and changed into battered old demireps in their twenties; adult suffrage tore the mask from the fabulous public opinion and democracy which Lincoln be-

lieved in and made the centre of his millennial hopes;
statesmen found that the way to the Treasury bench
was to "stoke up" public meetings with bunk, and
get photographed smoking briarwood pipes or nurs-
ing babies whilst convincing the bankers and finan-
ciers that they could be trusted to change nothing;
dictators superseded parliaments all over Europe,
proscribing their enemies like Sulla, and organizing
troops of young ruffians armed with irrestible modern
weapons to impose their wills effectively: in short, all
the aberrations that can occur in the absence of a
common faith and code of honor occurred and are
still occurring, including a monstrous war which no
armistice can stop for longer than time enough for
the disillusioned combatants to be superseded by a
new generation of young dupes.

   This very one-sided statement leaves out all that
we have gained by our liberation from the pseudo-
religious superstitions and pseudo-decent taboos and
pruderies that had produced the reaction against
Jehovah. That reaction was so monstrously overdone
that, being itself a reaction, it produced a counter-
reaction which is now taking the upper hand. It is
not too much to say that St. Thomas Aquinas has
now a wider vogue as a fashionable philosopher than
he ever enjoyed before. The Church of England,
which disgraced itself utterly during the Four Years
War by turning its vestries into Jingo recruiting sta-
tions, has redeemed itself by behaving very much bet-

ter since the resumption of that war in 1939. Psychology, which had belied itself by treating belief in the existence of such a thing as a soul as quite as superstitious as a belief in the existence of God, is becoming really psychological, just as biology is becoming really biological. Even medicine is following the lead of Scott Haldane, and beginning to regard a healthy body as a product of a healthy mind instead of the other way about. Butler, could he revisit us, would no longer find himself a boycotted crank. Even my own claims to be a biologist might not now be received with contemptuous incredulity by the biological profession. Obviously a playwright working on the Shakesperean plane in the great laboratory of the world with its uncontrived conditions, its innumerable untampered-with animals (mostly human) under observation, and its recorded history as I am, must be a biologist. Anyhow he can claim to know as much about the origins of life as the professionals, this being exactly nothing.

When I said many years ago that the Holy Ghost is the sole survivor of the Trinity, and that it is far more scientific to describe Man as the Temple of the Holy Ghost than as an automaton made of a few chemicals in which some carbon got mixed accidentally, I was accused of advertising myself by uttering paradoxes of the same order as the statement that black is white, which is not a paradox but a lie. Now that I am old and obsolescent, young people who hap-

pen to have heard about the paradoxical Shaw from
their elders, and are tempted to read him, cannot
find anything startling in me. If they have the requisite erudition, they point out that what I have said
had been said long ago by St. Augustine and all the
great spiritual leaders of mankind before and after
him. They class me as a Quaker of sorts, and are not
puzzled as their fathers were by the fact that Sir
Arthur Eddington, great as an astronomer, is a professed Friend, that Faraday and Darwin were members of religious sects, and that the now somewhat
forgotten Lucretian Irishman Tyndall, who startled
the world at Belfast in 1874 by declaring that he saw
greater advance than their grandfathers' discovery
that there is no such person as Old Nick with his
horns, tail, cloven hoof, and pitchfork. As to the belief of the physicists, which so discouraged Dean Inge,
one of the best brains of my time, that the sun is cool-
ing and the earth must therefore end as a frozen lifeless moon strewn with the bones of the Last Men, Sir
James Jeans, our Superphysicist, has suggested that
in matter the promise and potency of all forms of life,
is represented today by De Broglie, who scandalizes
nobody by demonstrating what was plain enough to
me in my teens: to wit, that if a dissolved salt can
crystallize itself into a solid stone it is as much alive
as the nearest squalling baby.

The Materialists, in fact, are faced with the discovery that there is no such thing as matter: a much

the continuous slowing down of the heavenly bodies
by the tides must finally stop them in their orbits,
whereupon, I suppose, they will all crash into one
another as disabled airplanes crash to earth, and
form a giant globe at a temperature never before
reached, in which life will carry on its work just as it
does on the floor of the ocean under pressures that no
dryland animal could endure for a moment.

It is a great relief to me to find that even the choice
spirits among the college professors (still a literally
Godforsaken lot) are ceasing to parrot obvious anti-
clerical nonsense in the firm belief that they are
teaching science. Imagine my delight when I received a copy of the first edition of this book inscribed
by its author as "an instalment of interest on an old
debt." His name being unknown to me, I hastened to
ascertain whether his chair was at Oxford or Cambridge, Owen's or Edinburgh, Dublin or Birming-
ham. I learnt that it was at Saskatoon, a place of
which I had never heard, and that his university was
that of Saskatchewan, which was connected in my
imagination with ochred and feathered Indians
rather than with a university apparently half a century ahead of Cambridge in science and of Oxford
in common sense.

Now I had noticed for some years past that American culture, which forty years ago seemed to subsist
mentally on stale British literary exports, was more
and more challenging our leadership, especially in

science. When I learned that provincial Canada had drawn easily ahead of Pasteurized Pavloffed Freudized Europe, and made professors of men who were in the vanguard instead of among the stragglers and camp followers, I found myself considering seriously, especially when the German airmen dropped a bomb near enough to shake my house, whether I had not better end my days in Vancouver, if not in Saskatoon. Meanwhile I urged, as strongly as I could, the reprinting of Professor Wilson's treatise in a modestly priced edition baited for the British book market with a preface by myself: an overrated attraction commercially, but one which still imposes on London publishers.

But I did not look at it commercially. I had an axe of my own to grind; and I thought Professor Wilson's book might help me to grind it. I am not a professor of language: I am a practitioner, concerned with its technique more directly than with its origin. Professor Wilson described how Man was a baby, to whom Time and Space meant no more than the present moment and the few feet in front of his nose, until writable language made Time historical and Thought philosophical. Thought lives on paper by the pen, having devised for itself an immortal and evergrowing body. You will understand this when you have read the book; and I hope you will appreciate its importance, and the magnitude of the service its author has done you.

Meanwhile, where do I come in? Solely as a technician. Professor Wilson has shewn that it was as a reading and writing animal that Man achieved his human eminence above those who are called beasts. Well, it is I and my like who have to do the writing. I have done it professionally for the last sixty years as well as it can be done with a hopelessly inadequate alphabet devised centuries before the English language existed to record another and very different language. Even this alphabet is reduced to absurdity by a foolish orthography based on the notion that the business of spelling is to represent the origin and history of a word instead of its sound and meaning. Thus an intelligent child who is bidden to spell debt, and very properly spells it d-e-t, is caned for not spelling it with a b because Julius Cæsar spelt the Latin word for it with a b.

Now I, being not only a scribe but a dramatic poet and therefore a word musician, cannot write down my word music for lack of an adequate notation. Composers of music have such a notation. Handel could mark his movements as *maestoso,* Beethoven as *mesto,* Elgar as *nobilemente,* Strauss, as *etwas ruhiger, aber trotzdem schwungvoll und enthusiastich.* By writing the words *adagio* or *prestissimo* they can make it impossible for a conductor to mistake a hymn for a hornpipe. They can write *ritardando, accellerando* and *tempo* over this or that passage. But I may have my best scenes ridiculously ruined in performance for want of such indications. A few nights ago I heard a broadcast recital of The Merchant of Venice in which Portia rattled through "How all the other passions fleet to air!" exactly as if she were still chatting with Nerissa and had been told by the producer to get through quickly, as the news had to come on at nine o'clock sharp. If that high spot in her part had been part of an opera composed by Richard Strauss a glance at the score would have saved her from throwing away her finest lines.

These particular instances seem impertinent to Professor Wilson's thesis; but I cite them to shew why, as a technician, I am specially concerned with the fixation of language by the art of writing, and hampered by the imperfections of that art. The Professor's conspectus of the enormous philosophical scope of the subject could not condescend to my petty everyday workshop grievances; but I may as well seize the opportunity to ventilate them, as they concern civilization to an extent which no layman can grasp. So let me without further preamble come down to certain prosaic technical facts of which I have to complain bitterly, and which have never as far as I know been presented in anything like their statistical magnitude and importance.

During the last 60 years I have had to provide for publication many millions of words, involving for me the manual labor of writing, and for the printer the setting up in type, of tens of millions of letters, largely superfluous. To save my own time I have resorted to shorthand, in which the words are spelt phonetically, and the definite and indefinite articles, with all the prepositions, conjunctions and interjections, as well as the auxiliary verbs, are not spelt at all, but indicated by dots and ticks, circles or segments of circles, single strokes of the pen and the like. Commercial correspondence is not always written: it is often spoken into dictaphones which cost more than most private people can afford. But whether it is dictaphoned or written in shorthand it has to be transcribed in ordinary spelling on typewriters, and, if for publication, set up from the typed copy on a printing machine operated by a stroke of the hand for every letter.

When we consider the prodigious total of manual labor on literature, journalism, and commercial correspondence that has to be done every day (a full copy of the London Times when we are at peace and not short of paper may contain a million words) the case for reducing this labor to the lowest possible figure is, for printers and authors, overwhelming, though for lay writers, most of whom write only an occasional private letter, it is negligible. Writers' cramp is a common complaint among authors: it does not trouble blacksmiths.

In what directions can this labor be saved? Two are obvious to anyone interested enough to give half an hour's thought to the subject. 1. Discard useless grammar. 2. Spell phonetically.

Useless grammar is a devastating plague. We who speak English have got rid of a good deal of the grammatic inflections that make Latin and its modern dialects so troublesome to learn. But we still say I am, thou art, he is, with the plurals we are, you are, they are, though our countryfolk, before school teachers perverted their natural wisdom, said I be, thou be, he be, we be, you be, they be. This saved time in writing and was perfectly intelligible in speech. Chinese traders, Negroes, and aboriginal Australians, who have to learn English as a foreign language, simplify it much further, and have thereby established what they call business English, or, as they pronounce it, Pidgin. The Chinese, accustomed to an uninflected monosyllabic language, do not say "I regret that I shall be unable to comply with your request." "Sorry no can" is quite as effective, and saves the time of both parties. When certain Negro slaves in America were oppressed by a lady planter who was very pious and very severe, their remonstrance, if expressed in grammatic English, would have been "If we are to be preached at let us not be flogged also: if we are to be flogged let us not be preached at also." This is correct and elegant but wretchedly feeble. It says in twenty-six words what can be better said in eleven. The Negroes proved this by saying "If preachee preachee: if floggee floggee; but no preachee floggee too." They saved fifteen words of useless grammar, and said what they had to say far more expressively. The economy in words: that is, in time, ink and paper, is enormous. If during my long professional career every thousand words I have written could have been reduced to less than half that number, my working lifetime would have been doubled. Add to this the saving of all the other authors, the scribes, the printers, the paper millers, and the makers of the machines they wear out; and the figures become astronomical.

However, the discarding of verbal inflections to indicate moods, tenses, subjunctives, and accusatives, multiplies words instead of saving them, because their places have to be taken by auxiliaries in such a statement as "By that time I shall have left England." The four words "I shall have left" can be expressed in more inflected languages by a single word. But the multiplication of words in this way greatly facilitates the acquisition of the language by foreigners. In fact, nearly all foreigners who are not professional interpreters or diplomatists, however laboriously they may have learnt classical English in school, soon find when they settle in England that academic correctness is quite unnecessary, and that "broken English," which is a sort of home made pidgin, is quite sufficient for intelligible speech. Instead of laughing at them and mimicking them derisively we should learn from them.

In acquiring a foreign language a great deal of trouble is caused by the irregular verbs. But why learn them? It is easy to regularize them. A child's "I thinked" instead of "I thought" is perfectly intelligible. When anybody says "who" instead of "whom" nobody is the least puzzled. But here we come up against another consideration. "Whom" may be a survival which is already half discarded: but nothing will ever induce an archbishop to say at the lectern "Who hath believed our report? and to who is the arm of the Lord revealed?"

But it is not for the sake of grammar that the superfluous m is retained. To pronounce a vowel we have to make what teachers of singing call a stroke of the glottis. The Germans, with their characteristic thoroughness, do this most conscientiously: they actually seem to like doing it; but the English, who are lazy speakers, grudge doing it once, and flatly refuse to do it twice in succession. The Archbishop says "To whom is" instead of "to who is" for the same reason as the man in the street, instead of saying Maria Ann, says Maria ran. The double *coup de glotte* is too troublesome. No Englishman, clerical or lay, will say "A ass met a obstacle." He says "A nass met a nobstacle." A Frenchman drops the final t in *"s'il vous plaît,"* but pronounces it in "plaît-il?" Euphony and ease of utterance call for such interpolations.

I can give no reason for the Cockney disuse of final l. Shakespear, accustomed to be called Bill by Anne

Hathaway, must have been surprised when he came to London to hear himself called Beeyaw, just as I was surprised when I came to London from Ireland to hear milk called meeyock. Final r does not exist in southern English speech except when it avoids a *coup de glotte*. In that case it is even interpolated, as in "the idear of." French, as written and printed, is plastered all over with letters that are never sounded, though they waste much labor when they are written.

The waste of time in spelling imaginary sounds and their history (or etymology as it is called) is monstrous in English and French; and so much has been written on the subject that it is quite stale, because the writers have dwelt only on the anomalies of our orthography, which are merely funny, and on the botheration of children by them. Nothing has been said of the colossal waste of time and material, though this alone is gigantic enough to bring about a reform so costly, so unpopular, and requiring so much mental effort as the introduction of a new alphabet and a new orthography. It is true that once the magnitude of the commercial saving is grasped the cost shrinks into insignificance; but it has not been grasped because it has never yet been stated in figures, perhaps because they are incalculable, perhaps because if they were fully calculated, the statisticians might be compelled to make the unit a billion or so, just as the astronomers have been compelled to make their unit of distance a lightyear.

In any case the waste does not come home to the layman. For example, take the two words tough and cough. He may not have to write them for years, if at all. Anyhow he now has tough and cough so thoroughly fixed in his head and everybody else's that he would be set down as illiterate if he wrote tuf and cof; consequently a reform would mean for him simply a lot of trouble not worth taking. Consequently the layman, always in a huge majority, will fight spelling reform tooth and nail. As he cannot be convinced, his opposition must be steam-rollered by the overworked writers and printers who feel the urgency of the reform.

Though I am an author, I also am left cold by tough and cough; for I, too, seldom write them. But take the words though and should and enough: containing eighteen letters. Heaven knows how many hundred thousand times I have had to write these constantly recurring words. With a new English alphabet replacing the old Semitic one with its added Latin vowels I should be able to spell t-h-o-u-g-h with two letters, s-h-o-u-l-d with three, and e-n-o-u-g-h with four: nine letters instead of eighteen: a saving of a hundred per cent of my time and my typist's time and the printer's time, to say nothing of the saving in paper and wear and tear of machinery. As I have said, I save my own time by shorthand; but as it all has to go into longhand before it can be printed, and I cannot use shorthand for my holograph epistles, shorthand is no remedy. I also have the personal grievance, shared by all my namesakes, of having to spell my own name with four letters instead of the two a Russian uses to spell it with his alphabet of 35 letters. All round me I hear the corruption of our language produced by the absurd device of spelling the first sound in my name with the two letters sh. London is surrounded by populous suburbs which began as homes or "hams" and grew to be hamlets or groups of hams. One of them is still called Peter's Ham, another Lewis Ham. But as these names are now spelt as one word this lack of a letter in our alphabet for the final sound in wish, and our very misleading use of sh to supply the deficiency, has set everyone calling them Peter Sham and Louis Sham. Further off, in Surrey, there is a place named Cars Halton. Now it is called Car Shallton. Horse Ham is called Hor-shm. Colt Hurst, which is good English, is called Coal Thirst, which is nonsense. For want of a letter to indicate the final sound in Smith we have Elt Ham called El Tham. We have no letter for the first and last consonant in church, and are driven to the absurd expedient of representing it by ch. Some-day we shall have Chichester called Chick Hester. A town formerly known as Sisseter is so insanely mis-spelt that it is now called Siren.

But the lack of consonants is a trifle beside our lack of vowels. The Latin alphabet gives us five, whereas the least we can write phonetically with is eighteen. I do not mean that there are only eighteen vowels in daily use: eighteen hundred would be nearer the truth. When I was chairman of the Spoken English Committee of the British Broadcasting Corporation it was easy enough to get a unanimous decision that exemplary and applicable should be pronounced with the stress on the first syllable, though the announcers keep on putting the stress on the second all the same; but when the announcers asked us how they should pronounce cross or launch there were as many different pronunciations of the vowels as there were members present. I secured a decision in favor of my own pronunciation of launch by the happy accident that it was adopted by King George the Fifth when christening a new liner on the Clyde. But the members were perfectly intelligible to one another in spite of their ringing all the possible changes between crawz and cross, between lanch and lawnch. To get such common words as son and science phonetically defined was hopeless. In what is called the Oxford accent son and sun became san; sawed and sword are pronounced alike; and my native city becomes Dabblin. In Dublin itself I have heard it called Dawblin. The Oxford pronunciation of science is sah-yence: the Irish pronunciation is sŭ-yence. Shakespear pronounced wind as wined; and as late as the end of the eighteenth century an attempt to correct an actor who pronounced it in this way provoked the retort "I cannot finned it in my minned to call it winned."

Rosalind is on the stage ridiculously pronounced
Rozzalinned though Shakespear called her Roh-za-
lined, rhyming it to "If a cat will after kind." Kind,
by the way, should logically be pronounced kinned.
The word trist is again so far out of use that nobody
knows how to pronounce it. It should rhyme to triced,
but is mostly supposed to rhyme to kissed. The first
vowel in Christ and Christendom has two widely different sounds, sometimes absurdly described as long i
and short i; but both are spelt alike.

I could fill pages with instances; but my present
point is not to make lists of anomalies, but to shew
that (a) the English language cannot be spelt with
five Latin vowels, and (b) that though the vowels
used by English people are as various as their faces
yet they understand one another's speech well enough
for all practical purposes, just as whilst Smith's face
differs from Jones's so much that the one could not
possibly be mistaken for the other yet they are so alike
that they are instantly recognizable as man and man,
not as cat and dog. In the same way it is found that
though the number of different vowel sounds we utter
is practically infinite yet a vowel alphabet of eighteen
letters can indicate a speech sufficiently unisonal to
be understood generally, and to preserve the language from the continual change which goes on at
present because the written word teaches nothing as
to the pronunciation, and frequently belies it. Absurd
pseudo-etymological spellings are taken to be pho-

netic, very soon in the case of words that are seldom heard, more slowly when constant usage keeps tradition alive, but none the less surely. When the masses learn to read tay becomes tee and obleezh becomes oblydge at the suggestion of the printed word in spite of usage. A workman who teaches himself to read pronounces semi- as see my. I myself, brought up to imitate the French pronunciation of envelope, am now trying to say enn-velope like everybody else.

Sometimes the change is an aesthetic improvement. My grandfather swore "be the varchoo" of his oath: I prefer vert-yoo. Edge-i-cate is less refined than ed-you-cate. The late Helen Taylor, John Stuart Mill's stepdaughter, who as a public speaker always said Russ-ya and Pruss-ya instead of Rusher and Prussher, left her hearers awestruck. The indefinite article, a neutral sound sometimes called the obscure vowel, and the commonest sound in our language though we cannot print it except by turning an e upside down, was always pronounced by Mrs. Annie Besant, perhaps the greatest British oratress of her time, as if it rhymed with pay. In short, we are all over the shop with our vowels because we cannot spell them with our alphabet. Like Scott, Dickens, Artemus Ward and other writers of dialect I have made desperate efforts to represent local and class dialects by the twentysix letters of the Latin alphabet, but found it impossible and had to give it up. A well-known actor, when studying one of my cockney parts, had to copy it in ordinary spelling before he could learn it.

My concern here, however, is not with pronunciation but with the saving of time wasted. We try to extend our alphabet by writing two letters instead of one; but we make a mess of this device. With reckless inconsistency we write sweat and sweet, and then write whet and wheat, just the contrary. Consistency is not always a virtue; but spelling becomes a will o' the wisp without it. I have never had much difficulty in spelling, because as a child I read a good deal, and my visual memory was good; but people who do not read much or at all, and whose word memory is aural, cannot spell academically, and are tempted to write illegibly to conceal this quite innocent inability, which they think disgraceful because illiteracy was for centuries a mark of class.

But neither speech nor writing can now be depended on as class indexes. Oxford graduates and costermongers alike call the sun the san and a rose a rah-ooz. The classical scholar and Poet Laureate John Dryden said yit and git where we say yet and get: another instance of spelling changing pronunciation instead of simply noting it. The Duke of Wellington dropped the h in humble and hospital, herb and hostler. So did I in my youth, though, as we were both Irish, h-dropping as practised in England and France was not native to us. I still say onner and our instead of honour and hour. Everybody does. Probably before long we shall all sing "Be it ever so umbl there's no place like ome," which is easier and prettier than "Be it evvah sah-oo hambl *etc.*"

I have dealt with vowels so far; but whenever an Englishman can get in an extra vowel and make it a diphthong he does so. When he tries to converse in French he cannot say *coupé* or *entrez*: he says coopay and ongtray. When he is in the chorus at a performance of one of the great Masses—say Bach's in B minor—he addresses the Almighty as Tay instead of making the Latin e a vowel. He calls gold gah-oold. I pronounce it goh-oold. Price, a very common word, is sometimes prah-ees, sometimes prawce, sometimes proyce, and sometimes, affectedly, prace. That is why our attempts to express our eighteen vowels with five letters by doubling them will not work: we cannot note down the diphthongal pronunciation until we have a separate single letter for every vowel, so that we can stop such mispronunciations as reel and ideel for real and ideal, and write diphthongs as such. The middle sound in beat, spelt with two letters, is a single pure vowel. The middle sound in bite, also spelt with two letters, is a diphthong. The spelling l-i-g-h-t is simply insane.

The worst vulgarism in English speech is a habit of prefixing the neutral vowel, which phoneticians usually indicate by e printed upside down, to all the vowels and diphthongs. The woman who asks for "e kapp e te-ee" is at once classed as, at best, lower middle. When I pass an elementary school and hear the children repeating the alphabet in unison, and chanting unrebuked "Ah-yee, Be-yee, Ce-yee, De-yee" I am restrained from going in and shooting the teacher only by the fact that I do not carry a gun and by my fear of the police. Not that I cannot understand the children when they speak; but their speech is ugly; and euphony is very important. By all means give us an adequate alphabet, and let people spell as they speak without any nonsense about bad or good or right or wrong spelling and speech; but let them remember that if they make ugly or slovenly sounds when they speak they will never be respected. This is so well known that masses of our population are bilingual. They have an official speech as part of their company manners which they do not use at home or in conversation with their equals. Sometimes they had better not. It is extremely irritating to a parent to be spoken to by a child in a superior manner; so wise children drop their school acquirements with their daddies and mummies. All such domestic friction would soon cease if it became impossible for us to learn to read and write without all learning to speak in the same way.

And now what, exactly, do I want done about it? I will be quite precise. I want our type designers, or artist-calligraphers, or whatever they call themselves, to design an alphabet capable of representing the sounds of the following string of nonsense quite unequivocally without using two letters to represent one sound or making the same letter represent different sounds by diacritical marks. The rule is to be One Sound One Letter, with every letter unmistakably different from all the others. Here is the string of nonsense. An alphabet which will spell it under these conditions will spell any English word well enough to begin with.

Chang at leisure was superior to Lynch in his rouge, munching a lozenge at the burial in Merrion Square of Hyperion the Alien who valued his billiards so highly.

Quick! quick! hear the queer story how father and son one time sat in the house man to man eating bread and telling the tale of the fir on the road to the city by the sea following the coast to its fall full two fathoms deep. There they lived together served by the carrier, whose narrower mind through beer was sore and whose poor boy shivered over the fire all day lingering in a tangle of tactless empty instinct ineptly swallowing quarts of stingo.

As well as I can count, this sample of English contains 372 sounds, and as spelt above requires 504 letters to print it, the loss in paper, ink, wear and tear of machinery, compositors' time, machinists' time, and author's time being over 26%, which could be saved by the use of the alphabet I ask for. I repeat that this figure, which means nothing to the mass of people who, when they write at all, seldom exceed one sheet of notepaper, is conclusive for reform in the case of people who are writing or typing or printing all day. Calligraphers intelligent enough to grasp its importance will, if they have read these pages, rush to their drawing boards to seize the opportunity.

The first question that will occur to them is how many letters they will have to design; for it will seem only commonsense to retain the 26 letters of the existing alphabet and invent only the ones in which it is deficient. But that can only serve if every letter in the 26 is given a fixed and invariable sound. The result would be a spelling which would not only lead the first generation of its readers to dismiss the writers as crudely illiterate, but would present unexpected obscenities which no decent person could be induced to write. The new alphabet must be so different from the old that no one could possibly mistake the new spelling for the old.

This disposes of all the attempts at "simplified spelling" with the old alphabet. There is nothing for it but to design 24 new consonants and 18 new vowels, making in all a new alphabet of 42 letters, and use it side by side with the present lettering until the better ousts the worse.

The artist-calligraphers will see at first only an opportunity for 42 beautiful line drawings to make a printed book as decorative as a panel by Giovanni da Udine, and a handwritten sonnet as delightful visually as one by Michael Angelo, the most perfect of all calligraphers. But that will never do. The first step is to settle the alphabet on purely utilitarian lines and then let the artists make it as handsome as they can. For instance, a straight line, written with a single stroke of the pen, can represent four different consonants by varying its length and position. Put a hook at the top of it, and you have four more consonants. Put a hook at the lower end, and you have four more, and put hooks at both ends and you have another four; so that you have 16 consonants writable by one stroke of the pen. The late Henry Sweet, still our leading authority on British phonetics, begins his alphabet in this way, achieving at one stroke p, t, k, and ch; b, d, g (hard) and j; m, n, ng and the ni in companion; kw, r, Spanish double l and the r in superior. He takes our manuscript e and l (different lengths of the same sign) and gets f, s, and zh. Turning it backwards he gets v, z, and sh. He takes our c and o, and gets dh and th. A waved stroke gives him l; and thus, borrowing only four letters from our alphabet, he obtains the required 24 consonants, leaving 22 of our letters derelict. For vowels he resorts to long and short curves at two levels, with or without little circles attached before or after, and thus gets the requisite 18 new letters easily. Thus the utilitarian task of inventing new letters has already been done by a first rate authority. The artists have only to discover how to make the strokes and curves pleasing to the eye.

At this point, however, the guidance of Henry Sweet must be dropped; for when he had completed his alphabet he proceeded to bedevil it into an instrument for verbatim reporting, which is the art of jotting down, not all the sounds uttered by a public speaker, which is beyond manual dexterity, but enough of them to remind the practised reporter of the entire words. He writes zah and depends on his memory or on the context to determine whether this means exact or example or examine or exasperate or what not. After seven years' practice Sweet became so expert at this sort of guessing that the specimens he gives in his Manual of Current Shorthand (published by the Clarendon Press) are unreadable by anyone lacking that experience.

This is true of all reporting systems. There are dozens of them in existence; and they are all efficient enough; for the debates of Cromwell's Ironsides and the cross-examinations of St. Joan are on record. Charles Dickens was a competent verbatim reporter before any of the systems now in use were invented. Sweet's contractions and guessings were therefore quite superfluous: what was needed from him was an alphabet with which the English language could be unequivocally spelt at full length, and not a new reporting shorthand.

Now Sweet, being a very English Englishman, was extremely quarrelsome. Being moreover the brainiest Oxford don of his time, he was embittered by the contempt with which his subject, to say nothing of himself, was treated by his university, which was and

still is full of the medieval notion, valid enough for
King Richard Lionheart but madly out of date today,
that English is no language for a gentleman, and is
tolerable only as a means of communication with the
lower classes. His wrath fell on his forerunner Isaac
Pitman, whose shorthand he called the Pitfall system.
Pitman had anticipated Sweet's strokes; but he made
their interpretation depend on their thickness and
the direction in which they were written. Thus a
horizontal stroke meant k, and a vertical one t. The
strokes slanting halfway between meant p and ch.
The same strokes thickened gave him g, d, b, and j,
with the addition of r for ch written upward instead
of downward. Thus he got nine letters from the single
stroke, and would have got ten if an upstroke could
be thickened, which is not possible as a feat of pen-
manship. Sweet discarded these distinctions because,
as no two people write at the same slant, the stroke
should have only one meaning no matter at what slant
it is written. Making strokes at different slants is
drawing, not writing; and Sweet insisted that writing
must be *currente calamo:* hence he called his script
Current Shorthand. Thick and thin he discarded as
unpractical for upstrokes and pencil work. His getting rid of these elaborations was an important improvement. The distinctions he substituted were those
to which the old printed alphabet has accustomed us.

In it the stroke projects sometimes above the line of
writing as in the letter l, sometimes below it as in

the letter j, sometimes neither above nor below as in
the letter i, sometimes both above and below as in
our manuscript p, f and capital j. This gave Sweet
only four letters per simple stroke instead of Pitman's
nine; but four are more than enough. Also much of
the pen work imposed by our alphabet is unnecessary: for instance, m and w take twice as long to
write as l though they can be indicated quite as
briefly; and p and q could be indicated by their pro-
jecting strokes alone without attaching an n to the
p and an o to the q.

I take it then that the new English alphabet will
be based on Sweet, and not on Pitman, though I am
writing this preface in Pitman's shorthand and not in
Sweet's, having discarded Sweet's reporting contractions as unnecessary for my purpose and puzzling
for my transcriber. The designer of the new alphabet
will find that Sweet has done all the preliminary
study for him, and solved its utilitarian problems.

What remains to be done is to make the strokes
and hooks and curves and circles look nice. If very
young, the designer may ask me indignantly whether
I think of the beauty sought by artists as something
to be stuck on to the inventions of the pedant. In this
case it is. An architect has to make a house beautiful; but the house, if it is to be lived in, must be
dictated by the needs of its inhabitants and not by
the architect's fancies. The great printers, Jensen,
Caslon, Morris, did not invent letters: they made the

old ones pleasing as well as legible, and made books worth looking at as well as reading. What they did for the old alphabet their successors must do for the new. There is plenty of scope for invention as well as for decoration: for instance, Sweet's alphabet has no capitals nor has Pitman's. Neither has any italics. Since Morris revived printing as a fine art, scores of new types have come into the market. Morris himself designed several.

The new alphabet, like the old, will not be written as printed: its calligraphers will have to provide us with a new handwriting. Our present one is so unwritable and illegible that I am bothered by official correspondents asking me to write my name "in block letters, please," though a good handwriting is more legible and far prettier than block, in which the letters, being the same height, cannot give every word a characteristic shape peculiar to itself. Shakespeare's signature, though orthographically illegible, is, when once you have learnt it, much more instantaneously recognizable and readable than SHAKESPEARE, which at a little distance might be CHAMBERLAIN or any other word of eleven letters.

Other changes and developments in the use of language and the art of writing may follow the introduction of an English alphabet. There is, for instance, the Basic English of the Orthological Institute at 10, King's Parade, Cambridge, by which foreigners can express all their wants in England by learning 800

English words. It is a thought-out pidgin, and gets rid of much of our grammatical superfluities. The Institute is, as far as I know, the best live organ for all the cognate reforms, as the literary Societies and Academies do nothing but award medals and read historical and critical lectures to one another.

The various schools of shorthand teach new alphabets; but they are wholly preoccupied with verbatim reporting, which is a separate affair. Their triumphs are reckoned in words per minute written at speeds at which no language can be fully written at all. They train correspondence clerks very efficiently; but they should pay more attention to authors and others whose business it is to write, and who cannot carry secretaries or dictaphones about with them everywhere. Such scribes can write at their own pace, and need no reporting contractions, which only waste their time and distract their attention, besides presenting insoluble puzzles to the typist who has to transcribe them. I have long since discarded them. On these terms shorthand is very easy to learn. On reporting terms it takes years of practice to acquire complete efficiency and then only in cases of exceptional natural aptitude, which varies curiously from individual to individual.

The only danger I can foresee in the establishment of an English alphabet is the danger of civil war. Our present spelling is incapable of indicating the sounds of our words and does not pretend to; but the

new spelling would prescribe an official pronunciation. Nobody at present calls a lam a lamb or pronounces wawk and tawk as walk and talk. But when
the pronunciation can be and is indicated, the dis-
putable points will be small enough for the stupidest
person to understand and fight about. And the feroc-
ity with which people fight about words is astonish-
ing. In London there is a street labelled Conduit
Street. When the word conduit, like the thing, went
out of use, cabmen were told to drive to Cundit
Street. They are still so told by elderly gentlemen.
When modern electric engineering brought the word
into common use the engineers called it con-dew-it.

A savage controversy in the columns of The Times
ensued. I tried to restore good humor by asking
whether, if the London University decided to pay a
compliment to our Oriental dominions by calling one
of its new streets Pundit Street it would be spelt Pon-
duit Street. I had better have said nothing; for I was
instantly assailed as a profane wretch trifling with a
sacred subject. Englishmen may yet kill one another
and bomb their cities into ruin to decide whether
v-a-s-e spells vawz or vahz or vaiz. Cawtholic or
Kahtholic may convulse Ireland when the national
question is dead and buried. We shall all agree that
h-e-i-g-h-t is an orthographic monstrosity; but when
it is abolished and we have to decide whether the
official pronunciation shall be hite or hyth, there will
probably be a sanguinary class war; for in this case

the proletarian custom is more logical than the Oxford one.

Still, we must take that risk. If the introduction of an English alphabet for the English language costs a civil war, or even, as the introduction of summer time did, a world war, I shall not grudge it. The waste of war is negligible in comparison to the daily waste of trying to communicate with one another in English through an alphabet with sixteen letters missing. That must be remedied, come what may.

Ayot St. Lawrence

AUTHOR'S FOREWORD

IN THIS SMALL VOLUME, I HAVE ATTEMPTED A PHILO-
sophical exposition of language. To have called it the
psychology, or the science, of language would have
been more in the fashion of the times, but I choose
"philosophy" as being both the more accurate and
the more comprehensive term.

I have treated language as one step or cycle in the
general evolution of the world, a cycle which includes
the following phases: the emergence of conscious
mind in the world and the new problem that emerged
with it; the birth of language in answer to this problem; the materials from which language was made;
the metamorphoses it underwent in reaching its final
form; its structure in relation to space and time; and
its unique character among other phenomena of the
world. A large undertaking, one might say, for so
small a volume; but whether I have failed or succeeded does not depend upon the size of the book.

I have avoided technical terms wherever that could
be done without impairing the adequacy of the treatment, partly from personal preference, and partly to
avoid placing stumbling-blocks of that sort in the
way of the non-specialist readers who might be interested in the subject. But though I have made the
treatment objective and concrete in order to make it

as simple and clear as possible, I have not wittingly sacrificed anything in order to make it popular. Whatever imperfections may be found in the treatment will be due to other causes than the concrete diction.

I wish to acknowledge my great indebtedness to my lifelong friend Mr. James Duff, M.A., formerly Chief Inspector of Schools in Saskatchewan, and now resident in Sidney, B. C. In addition to many conversations on various aspects of the subject, and subsequent frequent correspondence, he read over the final draft of the manuscript, with minute care, and suggested many modifications of thought or expression that were most valuable. My thanks are due also to my friend Mr. G. Kenderdine, who made the drawings to illustrate the correspondence and the difference between the world of natural objects and the world which is actualized by language. For permission to use copyright quotations thanks are due to Professor Julian Huxley and Basil Blackwell Ltd. for the verses from *The Captive Shrew;* Macmillan & Co. Ltd. for the extracts from Archbishop Bernard's translation of Kant's *Critique of Judgment;* the executors of the late A. F. Murison for his translation of the *Ode* from Horace; and McClelland & Stewart of Toronto and the author's executors for the lines from *The Choristers* from *Poems* by Bliss Carman.

I am gratefully indebted to Mr. Bernard Shaw for the interest he has taken in the book and especially for his most generous action in taking the time from his crowded life to write so magnanimous and stimulating a Preface to it.

University of Saskatchewan

SECTION I

CLEARING THE WAY

CHAPTER I

THE AIM, AND THE METHOD
OF TREATMENT

But that same Where (Space), with its brother
When (Time), are from the first the master-colours
of our Dream-Grotto; the Canvas (the warp and woof
thereof) whereon all our Dreams and Life-Visions are
painted.—CARLYLE, *Sartor Resartus*, 1830.

❖   ❖   ❖   ❖

WHEN KANT IN HIS INVESTIGATION OF THE NATURE
and validity of human knowledge in the *Critique of
Pure Reason* (1781) undertook an examination of the
nature of Space and Time as the starting point in the
discussion, he struck the path which all fruitful philosophical investigation has followed since. Since Space
and Time are the two "forms" within which the
whole system of life and nature unfolds itself to the
human mind, and are at the same time the "warp
and woof" on which man elaborates his mental sense-
picture of the world, an examination of these two
sense-forms should be the self-evident starting point
in any true cosmic philosophy. Yet it seems to have
taken something more than a century for the full
significance of Kant's method to sink into the general
philosophical consciousness, and it is only in our own
time that its fruits have begun to mature. What

53

strikes one in the philosophical writings of the present century, whether starting from mathematics, or science, or pure speculation, is the common assumption in all of them that some exposition of Space and Time must form the foundation of any adequate treatment of the nature of the world, the human mind, and the structure of human knowledge. The title of Professor Alexander's book, *Space, Time, and Deity*, is symbolic of the modern point of view.

From these modern philosophical treatises, however, one significant human phenomenon has been omitted—language. So far as I know no attempt has been made to explore the nature of language in relation to space and time. And yet among the "novelties" which "emerged" to actuality with man's emergence from the realm of nature into the realm of free mind, language is the most distinctive and significant. It is the one unique human instrument which man has designed for the purpose of elaborating within his own mind an actual mental picture of the material world of Space and Time in which he lives. By means of these designed symbols of language he has built up and is still building up within his own mind a space-time picture of the space-time world; and since the space-time mental picture elaborated by language is the approximating image or counterpart of the actual space-time world, there must be a close correspondence between the structure of language and the structure of the world which language images. It seems probable, therefore, that an examination of the structure and significance of language in relation to Space and Time may bring to light certain characteristics of language, and of the human mind that created it, that are not otherwise apparent. It is in this hope that the present investigation has been undertaken.

To work the problem out adequately, however, some preliminary clearing of the way will be necessary. This preliminary work will include three things: first, a very brief statement and exposition of the old Hebrew theory of language origin; second, a short reference to Plato's theory as being the first freely scientific and radical treatment of the question; and third, an outline of the development of modern language theory from the publication of Herder's radical essay in 1772 to the publication of Darwin's *Descent of Man* in 1871, when the stream of modern philosophic thought regarding the origin and meaning of language was deflected so violently from its natural course that it has not recovered since.

Because of this deflection I shall take 1871 as the starting point in time for the development of my own view. In this, the main part of the work, I shall give first of all a statement and criticism of Darwin's view, and then, using this as a logical starting point, I shall attempt a new philosophical exposition of the origin and structure of language in relation to the two sense-forms of Space and Time.

CHAPTER II

TWO OLD-WORLD THEORIES
OF LANGUAGE

Adam's first task was giving names to natural Appearances: what is ours still but a continuation of the same?—CARLYLE, *Sartor Resartus*, 1830.

❖   ❖   ❖   ❖

1. *The Genesis Theory* (*c.* 950 B.C.)

WHAT IS NOW USUALLY KNOWN AS THE "EXTERNAL divine-origin theory" of language—a misnomer which arose from erroneous theological expositions of the narrative given in the early chapters of Genesis—has still an interest for the modern student; first, because of the prolonged influence which it has had upon language theory in the Western world; and second, because of certain significant facts regarding language which an understanding reader still finds in that old story of language origin, to say nothing of the poetic attractiveness of the story itself.

The Hebrew writer of the Genesis narrative had observed the fact that of the gifts which God had bestowed on man language was one of the most significant. Man had come into possession of the unique power of naming and classifying the things of the world; and in attempting an explanation of how this naming process was actually accomplished that early writer put it in the following manner: "And out of the ground the Lord God formed every beast of the field, and every fowl of the air; and brought them unto Adam to see what he would call them; and whatsoever Adam called every living creature, that was the name thereof. And Adam gave names to all cattle, and to the fowl of the air, and to every beast of the field." That is the Hebrew writer's brief and naïve story of the birth of language; a story which the modern child of ten years will still accept at literal face value, which the man of twenty who puts away childish things will reject, and which the philosopher of forty, who has grown in discernment as well as in knowledge, will reaccept with some surprise at the amount of factual truth contained in it. We do not think now, of course, that the naming of living things in the world happened in such a summary matter-of-fact fashion as that, and yet there are three things in this old account that have significance still to the modern scientist, despite the new views about language which have become orthodox since 1871.

First. Whether it was that the animals were brought to man, or that man went to the animals, or that they mutually confronted each other—the method of early poetic statement of the fact matters little—the result was that man *did* name the animals; and the fact of his naming them indicated that he had come into possession of this unique power of language which the animals apparently did not have, because they had not given names to themselves or to one another. Furthermore, this record of man's having named the animals of the world was written some three thousand-odd years ago, and the animals have not yet made any start at naming themselves. This difference between man and the animals as evidenced in man's power of giving names, and thus making explicit classification of things, is a unique difference between the two, a difference whose significance has not yet been clearly brought out in modern discussions of the subject. In fact, since Darwin's formulation of the evolutionary theory in reference to man in 1871, the difference has been persistently either obscured or denied altogether.

Second. According to this old writer's account, man's first interest was with the world of living things rather than with insentient life or inanimate nature. "Adam gave names to all cattle, and to the fowl of the air, and to every beast of the field." No mention is made of the naming of trees, or plants, or inanimate objects. This furnishes no conclusive evidence, of course, of the actual order in which man named the things of the world; but the things which the first writer observed as having been named by Adam were very probably the things that first interested man and induced him to mark their differences by giving them names. At all events, the passage has interest as giving

us one of the earliest records of man's first impression
about the matter.

Third. This writer saw also that when the name
was once given to the animal it stuck to him. "Whatsoever name Adam called every living creature, that
was the name thereof." Some of these names given
in the remote beginnings of the Semitic language,
long before the Genesis record was written, have, as
a matter of fact, stuck to these animals down to the
present time; though countless generations of the
animals themselves have come into being and disappeared again in a continuously vanishing stream.
The giving of the name was thus the introduction of
a new element into the world, the element of *permanence* which persists through the series of un-perma-
nent things. This permanent element, as I hope to
show later, belongs in its explicit form to the mind of
man alone, and takes on its adequate outward form
in language.

In interpreting the old Genesis story in this explicit modern way one may be guilty of discovering
more in it than the author intentionally put there;
though one who has been trained in the literalism
of Western thought and expression is seldom sure
whether he is finding too much or too little in even
the simplest objective symbolism of the East, as in
the older portions of the Bible. In any case, to have
observed and recorded the fact of this sticking power
of names in contrast to the vanishing series of things

that are named, was a distinct achievement or lucky hit for so early a thinker and, when adequately interpreted, turns out to be a permanent contribution to the philosophy of language. But we shall have occasion to revert to this a little farther on.

The Genesis writer had also observed the diversity of languages in the world, and ventured an explanation of this. Originally, he says, "the whole world was of one language and of one speech." But when God saw that by the use of this single language man aspired "to build a city and a tower whose top may reach unto heaven," He "confounded their language so that they might not understand one another's speech," and "scattered them abroad from thence upon the face of the earth." The "city and tower" was obviously used by the writer as a figure to symbolize the inordinate vanity of man's knowledge and power, and since language was man's prime instrument for the realization of his ambitious aims, his vanity could be most effectively curbed by the confusion of his language. This whole explanatory story is based upon a purely moral conception of the world, and was no doubt a very plausible explanation at a time when the man-inhabited world was conceived as a relatively small place, and man's sojourn on it of relatively short duration.

This Genesis account of the beginnings and diversity of language when looked at in a sensible way is really quite a natural one, though the naïve statement that God brought the animals to Adam, as one person might bring them to another, indicates a point of view quite different from the modern. It was Adam, however, according to the narrative, who actually did the naming, that is, who actually made the first words of language. In the process of time, however, theological preconception and prejudice gradually shifted the emphasis from Adam to God, and interpreted the story as meaning that language was a direct and ready-made gift from God to man.

From the modern point of view this theological explanation of language origin and vicissitudes has turned out to be unsatisfactory, but it is interesting as showing man's very early interest in the problem and some of his first guesses about it. It is significant also from the fact that it was the generally accepted language-origin theory up until the middle of the eighteenth century.

2. *Plato* (427–347 B.C.)

Plato's theory of language origin requires mention here, though for valid reasons its exposition will be postponed to another place. The Hebrew writer of the Genesis narrative gave us merely a factual statement of language origin. While the facts which he noted are, as we saw, significant, he attempted no scientific or metaphysical exposition of them. Plato, on the other hand, accepts the facts of language as given, starting, as it were, where the Hebrew account leaves off, and then asks the question: "How did the facts of language come about?" or more specifically: "How were the first words of language actually made, and what was the principle which operated in and guided the process of making?" His approach to the question was entirely radical, and his treatment of it in the *Cratylus,* which, as usual with Plato, is a compound of science and philosophy, is on the whole more fundamental and adequate than any modern treatment of the subject that I know. Emerson once spoke of the "perpetual modernness" of Plato's dialogues. As with the other dialogues this perpetual modernness lifts the *Cratylus* quite above the stream of historical treatises upon language origin which we are discussing in this section, and makes it contemporary with the best modern discussions of the subject. Hence the examination of Plato's theory will be postponed until we come to the specific question of the actual beginnings of language which must be the subject of another volume.

Plato, however, was aware of a prime difficulty in his quest of language origin in not having an adequate body of foreign-language material for purpose of comparative study. Socrates, who leads the discussion, frequently comes across a word which is obviously not of Greek origin. These words, he says, must have been imported by the Greeks from their barbarian neighbours, and he makes in one place the significant remark, from the point of view of language study, that "the barbarians are older than we are." He points out that to give a complete account of language origin these words of foreign source would have to be traced home to their original forms in the language of the people who made them, but the Greeks had no knowledge of the language of their barbarian neighbours to enable them to carry out this investigation. Plato, with respect to this difficulty, was in the same position as were Herder and other early modern investigators of language prior to Sir William Jones's discovery of Sanskrit in the seventeen-eighties.

CHAPTER III

ROUSSEAU (1712-72): THE OLD AND THE NEW

❖   ❖   ❖   ❖

DURING THE MIDDLE AGES AND UP TO THE MIDDLE of the eighteenth century, the theologians' mutilated version of the Genesis account of language origin, the divine-origin theory as it came to be called, was the theory held by Christian Europe. In the eighteenth century, however, the question of the probability of a natural rather than a supernatural origin of language began to stir in men's minds. Rousseau's essay on the *Origin of Languages,* about 1750, might be taken as the historical landmark which stands between the old and new points of view. This essay is in itself disappointing to one who is acquainted with Rousseau's other works. His mental interests were practical rather than speculative, and he had no real convictions about the question of language as he had about education, society, and government. He was interested in language, and the changes in language, in relation to the practical needs of the people in social and national groups, and in diverse climatic conditions, rather than in the origin of language itself as an instrument of human reason. As a consequence his essay on the *Origin of Languages*—not "Language"—is hardly more than a series of disconnected reflections upon various aspects of languages, including a discussion of the relation of language to melody and harmony in music which occupies about one-third of the essay.

There is a curious inconsistency in the essay, which, in so far as Rousseau can be accepted as a representative of the current thought of time, may mark historically the last association of the theological and the philosophical conceptions of language in a single treatise, on the eve of the final parting of their ways. Rousseau admits, in at least a lukewarm fashion, the divine-origin theory of language: "Adam spake; very well: Adam had been taught by God Himself. . . . It is easy to reconcile the authority of the Scripture with the monuments of antiquity, and one is not reduced to treating as fables traditions as old as the people who transmitted them to us." His own independent comments, however, all point to a natural origin of language, though he did not develop them with sufficient philosophic acumen to be of much value to a modern student of language. The sentence by which he closes the essay might be taken quite literally as a fair judgment of the philosophical value of his work, and as showing also, in his quotation from M. Duclos, the source and nature of his own interest in language: "I shall close these superficial reflections, but from which others more profound may arise, by a passage from M. Duclos, which suggested them to me: 'It would be the subject of a very philosophical examination to show by examples how much the character, the morals, and the interests of a people influence their language.' " Rousseau's essay has interest for the modern student rather as a historical signpost than as a philosophical exposition. It stands, as I have said, between the old world and the new, and I have allowed a chapter to Rousseau's name to mark symbolically his position between the two worlds.

CHAPTER IV

HERDER AND THE NEW WORLD

> In Being's floods, in Action's storm,
> I walk and work, above, beneath,
> Work and weave in endless motion!
> > Birth and Death,
> > And infinite ocean;
> > A seizing and giving
> > The fire of living.
> 'Tis thus at the roaring Loom of Time I ply,
> And weave the living Robe of Deity.

> > > GOETHE, Song of the Earth-Spirit, *Faust,* 1774.

❖   ❖   ❖   ❖

1. *The New-World View*

IF PRESSED FOR AN EXACT DATE OF THE TRUE BEGIN-
ning of the scientific investigation of language, one
would naturally think of the date of the publication of Johann Gottfried Herder's prize essay on the
Origin of Language, 1772. In passing from Rousseau's essay to Herder's—although they are separated
by only twenty-two years, and by the distance between Paris and Strassburg—we step clearly over the
threshold from medievalism into the new world of
free philosophical investigation, into an atmosphere
as clear as that in which Plato and Aristotle worked.
Herder's essay on language is the starting point for
all the scientific work that has since been done on

that subject, and has thus a very important historical significance in addition to its permanent scientific value. Its full significance, however, can be fully appreciated only in relation to the general scientific and philosophic thought of the time, and it will be necessary to digress for a few pages to describe the intellectual atmosphere in which Herder worked in the latter half of the eighteenth century in Germany.

Professor Jespersen, in tracing the history of linguistic science in his recent book on the *Language, Its Nature, Development, and Origin,* says that: "The chief innovation of the beginning of the nineteenth century was the historical point of view . . . the application of the notion of history to other things than wars and the vicissitudes of dynasties, and the discovery of the idea of development or evolution as pervading the whole universe." This statement is in the broad sense true. Yet it must be remembered that while the thoroughgoing application of the principle of evolution to the many phases of existence was the achievement of the nineteenth century, the discovery of the principle as a directing agency in the world, together with its corollary or co-principle of the organic unity of the world, was really the discovery of the closing half of the eighteenth century. It was the central and stimulating idea in the scientific work of Erasmus Darwin (1731–1802) in Britain, and of Buffon (1707–88) and Lamarck (1744–1829) in France; and in the philosophy, science, and poetry of Kant (1724–1804), Herder (1744–1803), and Goethe (1749–1832) in Germany, to mention only the greatest names. The movement in Germany is our chief concern here. It was more comprehensive in scope than the movement in England and France, and had a greater influence upon the course of world thought in the nineteenth century; and Herder himself, whose essay on language is our main interest, bore an active part in it. His essay on language, however, was only a special phase of the general evolutionary theory of the world which was being formulated in the thought of the time, and the comments upon the general scientific and philosophic work of Kant, Goethe, and Herder in the next few paragraphs are given merely with a view to a better understanding of Herder's language essay.

2. *Kant* (1724–1804) *and Goethe* (1749–1832)

But here, as in so many other cases, Germany, learned, indefatigable, deep-thinking Germany, comes to our aid.— CARLYLE, *Sartor Resartus,* 1830.

Kant was a mathematician and scientist before he became a philosopher, and these pre-philosophical studies played a large part in shaping his philosophy. In his first important scientific work, the *General History of Nature and Theory of the Heavens,* 1755, he explained the present animate world as the result of a very long and gradual evolution, through natural causation, from the less to the more complex forms of life. To the general conception of evolution then gradually coming to view he contributed the original ideas of Selection, Adaptation, Environment, and Inheritance as essential factors in the general development. In his last significant philosophic work, *The Critique of Judgment,* 1790, which he designed and developed as the coping stone for his two former philosophical works, *The Critique of Pure Reason,* 1781, and *The Critique of Practical Reason,* 1788, the conception of development is a dominating and shaping idea. Here, however, in his final views, he unites the law of natural causation with the teleological principle of final causes acting towards definite ends. Haeckel, in his estimate of Kant's work, considers this introduction of *purpose* into world-evolution as a retrograde step, on the part of Kant, from the views of natural causation developed in his *History of Nature* thirty-five years earlier. Kant, however, considered his final statement as the more comprehensive and logical, more in accordance with the entire phenomena of nature, life, and mind in the world. But the interesting part of the whole *Critique of Judgment* is the modernness of the conception of evolution developed in it. There is one paragraph in the book that might have been used by Darwin himself as a statement in outline of all that he afterwards worked out in detail in the *Origin of Species* (1859) and *Descent of Man* (1871). This paragraph alone would give us perhaps better than anything else we could find a clear image of the advanced scientific and philosophic thought of the time in Germany.

It is desirable [says Kant] to examine the great domain of organized beings, by means of comparative anatomy, in order to see whether we may not find in them something resembling a system, and indeed something in accordance with the principle of generation. Otherwise we would have to be content with a mere consideration of things as they are—which gives us no insight into their generation—and, in despair, give up all hope or claim of natural insight into this field. The agreement of so many genera of animals in a certain common plan of structure, which seems to be fundamental not only in the structure of their bones, but also in the arrangements of their other parts—so that with an admirable simplicity of original outline, a great variety of species has been produced by the shortening of one member and the lengthening of another, the involution of this part and the evolution of that—allows a ray of hope, however faint, to penetrate into our minds, that some results might be obtained here by the application of the principle of the mechanism of Nature, without which there can be no natural science at all. This analogy of forms, which with all their differences seem to have been produced according to a common original type, strengthens our surmise of an actual relationship among them in their procreation from a common parent, through the gradual approximation of one animal-genus to another—from that genus in which the principle of purposiveness seems best authenticated, namely man, down to the polyp, and again from this down to mosses and lichens, and finally to the lowest form of Nature observable to us, namely to raw matter. And so the whole technique of Nature, which, as perceived in organized beings, is so incomprehensible to us that we feel ourselves compelled to think a different principle for it, seems to have been derived from matter and its powers according to mechanical laws (like those which are operative in the formation of crystal).—KANT, *Critique of Judgment*, Bernard's translation, p. 337.

This was published, as we have said, in 1790, and this view of the organic unity of the diversified forms of the world, and their natural evolution from simple beginnings, together with the principle of purpose which Kant associated with it, constitutes the logical groundwork of the *Critique of Judgment*.

The same idea pervades the contemporary work of Goethe. "Goethe," says Professor Osborn, "was the greatest poet of Evolution; he saw the law as a poet, as a philosopher, and as an anatomist." His scientific work is very well known in a general way to those who have read the story of modern scientific thought; but as a recent visitor to Weimar says:

It is impossible to have an adequate conception of the part played by science in Goethe's life unless one has visited the Goethe house in Weimar. The place resembles a museum rather than a private home, and several large rooms of this museum contain nothing but the apparatus and materials which Goethe used in his scientific experimentation. Chemicals, rocks, and ores of all kinds, and many species of intricate instruments occupy table after table. But most surprising of all is Goethe's private library. One would expect to find there a rich collection of belles lettres; instead one finds the shelves lined with journals of chemistry, physics, geology, etc. It is only after such a visit that one appreciates

the many-sided thoroughness of that great mind.—STEIN-
HAUER.

Goethe was a lifelong student of science, and during his first Weimar period, from 1775 to 1786, his
interest was devoted almost exclusively to scientific
study: mineralogy, botany, geology, physiology, oste-
ology. He went to Jena for a course in anatomy under
Loder, and to perfect his own knowledge he gave
weekly lectures on the skeleton to the young men
there. His absorption in science caused great concern
to Herder and others of his friends in Weimar who
already knew his genius for poetry. But all these sys-
tematic studies over a dozen years were carried on
from a purely scientific curiosity to know how the
present world came to be what it is, and the idea of
evolution gave him the answer to the question. His
research in natural science alone would have given
him a place in modern thought had it not been over-
shadowed by his greater work in poetry.

He went to Italy in 1786, and it was during his
two years' stay there that his main interest was turned
back again from science to poetry. "I have aban-
doned," he writes from Italy, "my master Loder for
my friend Schiller, and Linnaeus for Shakespeare."
He saw perhaps, as Shakespeare did, that the poet
in his creative activity "shares with great creating
nature," and in his art, as nature's agent, may add
another rung to the ladder of evolution itself, while
science at best can only examine and tabulate the

rungs that are already set; and if, in his return to poetry, "science lost a disciple who would have ranked among the very highest, if not the highest," [1] the world, in compensation, has gained an edifice of art whose foundations are laid in the excavations of scientific research and whose upper structure will itself be the object of many scientific investigations in the future. Poetry deals primarily with human life; and with nature only as it affects the growth and course of human life. Even in his scientific years Goethe believed that "the chief study of Mankind is Man," but he saw that the roots of man's life are in nature, and his scientific research had a purpose in relation to his poetry. It gave a proportioned perspective to his view of life and the world as a whole, and gave depth and unity of design to his representations of life in both his verse and prose. If, as Schiller says of him, "his spirit works and seeks in every direction, *striving to create a whole,*" his scientific studies contributed not a little to that unifying impulse and vision. His work, as Carlyle pointed out, is significantly original and modern, the intellectual faculty as clear as the imaginative faculty is vivid. Everywhere in the world he saw development and evolution, not mechanical, but organic and vital. The song of the Earth-Spirit in *Faust,* quoted above, considered as a vital expression of the principle of development at work in the world, has not been surpassed by any-

[1] Osborn, *From the Greeks to Darwin,* p. 181.

thing of a similar kind and length in the nineteenth century. It is the core of his interpretation of life and the world.

3. *Herder* (1744–1803)

By his work on language, *Uber den Ursprung der Sprache* (1772), Herder may be said to have laid the first rude foundations of the science of comparative philology, and of that deeper science of the ultimate nature and origin of language.—J. SULLY (1911).

It was in this atmosphere that Herder lived. He was a student under Kant—who was twenty years his senior—at Königsberg between 1762 and 1764, and Kant's *History of Nature* had been published seven years before. He met and became an intimate friend of Goethe—who was five years his junior—at Strassburg in 1770, and from 1776 when Herder, through the influence of Goethe, moved to Weimar, the two men lived in more or less intimate contact with one another there until Herder's death in 1803. With the greatest scientist-philosopher on one side and scientist-poet on the other, and with his own native genius for science, literature, and philosophy, all working under the impulse of a new idea that promised to give unity to the whole world of nature and man, Herder's own contributions to the general movement had every likelihood of being important and unique. He absorbed Kant's ideas of evolution in nature, and in his own work, *Ideas for a Philosophy of the History*

of Mankind (1784–91), he carried them forward in
several important directions, notably by his development of the doctrine of the Unity of Type pervading
the entire animal world. The clearness of his grasp
of the general principle of evolution, and the significance of his own contributions to it may be estimated
by the fact that when F. von Barenach published his
exposition of Herder's works in 1877 he gave it the
title, *Herder as the Precursor of Darwin and Modern
Natural Philosophy*. From all this one can estimate
Herder's general equipment for the investigation of
language origin and development as a particular
phase of genesis and evolution; and since, as we have
said, his essay is the starting point of modern language study, it seemed worth while giving this space
to a description of the intellectual atmosphere out of
which it came.

His essay on language was stimulated chiefly by
Johann Peter Süssmilch's treatise on language in
1776, which was written with the purpose of proving
the orthodox view which was held generally up to
that time, that "human language is a direct gift from
God." Herder's primary object was to refute this
thesis by submitting evidence and argument to show
that language was invented and gradually perfected
by man as the natural means of developing his own
reason. He starts with a statement from Süssmilch
which Süssmilch claimed to have proved in his treatise, namely, that "the use of language is indispensable

for the use of reason," and he uses this statement as a basis for refuting Süssmilch's whole theory. He pointed out that when man, in the very first step of his reasoning power, had isolated one object of his environment from all other objects, this isolated object "retained in the mind, was a word in the soul. . . . With this first distinct concept of an object isolated from other objects, language was already in his soul, hence it was invented through his own resources and not in a mechanical manner through divine instructions. It was not God who invented language for man. Man himself had to invent language in exercising his own powers."

One of Herder's strong negative arguments against the divine origin of language was based upon "the imperfection of language." The fact, for example, that the Arab languages had a great many synonyms for common and familiar things—"fifty different names for the lion, two hundred for the snake, eighty for honey, seventy for a stone"—and was often lacking altogether in words for the expression of "difficult and rare ideas," shows that language was made by man in his own imperfect groping fashion, and not by God. This line of argument is interesting to the modern students as a record of the contemporary attitude of mind that had to be broken down before men could get forward in the natural investigation of language.

Herder's essay will always remain an important

document in the history of linguistic science for two reasons. First, for the preliminary clearing of the way which we have just mentioned above. He did effectively refute, once for all, the divine-origin theory of language, and make the way clear and open for the free scientific investigation of language which has gone on since the publication of his essay one hundred and sixty-five years ago. This was a very necessary piece of work at the time, even though it has little more than an historical interest for us now.

Second. Herder's real interest, however, was not in this negative work of refuting an inadequate theory, but in replacing it by a sound philosophical theory of his own. "If," says he, "it is incomprehensible to others how a human mind could invent language, it is incomprehensible to me how a human mind could be what it is without discovering language for itself." This is his starting point, and his long and closely written essay of some ninety-odd pages is so rich in evidence and suggestion regarding the natural origin and development of language that no serious modern student of language can afford to be unacquainted with it.

But, as already pointed out, for the successful investigation of the problem of language one requires an adequate body of concrete language data as well as a directing principle, and that body of fact was not available in 1772. Herder, who knew the contemporary data well, says in his essay that the language material of the various foreign peoples is as yet so meagre and unreliable that "an exact science of comparative language is not yet possible," so that despite his own great natural endowment he was in the position of a bird attempting a flight with one of its wings as yet inadequately feathered.

CHAPTER V

FROM HERDER TO DARWIN,
1772–1871

Nature leads the way. Man emerges on the scene, follows her footprints, marks and registers them in language, and makes a *Science of Nature*. Then he looks back and discovers that Language, while following the path of Nature, has left a trail of her own. He returns on this new trail, again marks and registers *its* footprints, and makes a *Science of Language*.

❖   ❖   ❖   ❖

The Discovery of Sanskrit and Comparative Philology

MY PURPOSE IN THIS BOOK IS NOT TO COMPARE LANguages as in linguistic science, or to trace their concrete development as in language history; but to describe the problem which gave birth to language, to show the place of language in the general scheme of world evolution, and to point out its basic structure in relation to the two forms of sense, Space and Time. I have dealt at some length with Herder and his time because that period was the beginning of the modern movement in language investigation in which we are still engaged. For the next hundred years, from Herder's essay in 1772 to Darwin's *Descent of Man* in 1871, I can only touch some of the peaks in the development of linguistic theory and science that, in their combined results, have prepared the way for the present inquiry, and that may help to give the perspective necessary to set the fabric of language clearly in its place among the other phenomena of the world. If this mode of treatment should appear to the language specialist as in some degree wanting in the "hard factualness" of language, the explanation is that the inclusion of such factual material would not contribute to the investigation in hand. If one can make clear the world-problem which called language into existence, and show the structure which language was destined to assume in order to answer this problem, then the way should be better prepared and the impulse quickened for tracing man's first steps and subsequent windings in the actual making of language.

Herder, as we saw, had a clear grasp of the general principle of evolution, but was handicapped in his application of the principle to language because of the lack of an adequate and trustworthy body of foreign language material in 1772. At the close of the century, however, while Herder was still living, that required material came to hand in a rather unexpected but quite natural way.

The struggle between the French and English in the eighteenth century for the possession of the territory and wealth of India brought a number of French and English scholars, who were connected with the military or civil occupation of India, into contact with the Sanskrit language. A French Jesuit missionary, Courdoux, sent a memoir to the French Institute in 1767, calling attention to numerous similarities between Sanskrit and Latin words, and also to certain similarities between the respective inflections of these words. His observations were not published, however, until forty years later, and meanwhile similar observations were made and announced by others.

The scholar whose name stands first among the introducers of Sanskrit and comparative linguistics into Europe is Sir William Jones (1746–94). He had shown a genius for language while a student at Harrow and Oxford, and at twenty-four had a mastery of ten foreign languages, including Hebrew, Arabic, and Persian. Though an accomplished classical scholar he had a preference for Oriental languages. He took up law as a means of livelihood, was called to the Bar in 1774, and in 1783 was appointed a judge of the Supreme Court at Calcutta. This gave him the opportunity he had been awaiting for the study of the Sanskrit language at first hand. In 1784, the year after his arrival in Calcutta, with the co-operation of Sir Charles Wilkins (1749–1836), "the first Englishman who acquired a critical knowledge of the Sanskrit language . . . and opened the mine of Sanskrit literature" (Sir W. Jones), he founded the Asiatic Society for the study of the language and literature of the East. This was an important event. "The history of what may be called European Sanskrit philology," says Max Müller, "dates from the foundation of the Asiatic Society at Calcutta in 1784." It was in his third address before this society, on 27th September 1786, *On the Hindus,* that Sir William Jones gave the memorable paragraph that became the starting point for the modern science of Comparative Philology in Europe.

The *Sanskrit* language [says he], whatever be its antiquity, is of a wonderful structure; more perfect than the Greek, more copious than the Latin, and more exquisitely refined than either; yet bearing to both of them a stronger affinity, both in the roots of verbs, and in the forms of grammar, than could possibly have been produced by accident; so strong indeed that no philologer could examine them all three without believing them to have sprung from *some common source*, which perhaps no longer exists. There is a similar reason, though not quite so forcible, for supposing that both the *Gothick* and the *Celtick*, though blended with a very different idiom, had the same origin with the Sanskrit; and the old *Persian* might be added to the same family.[1]

Sir William Jones did not live to carry out in detail the comparison which he here makes, but in this single paragraph he clearly formulated the conception which became the basis for the whole science of comparative linguistics, which was subsequently developed in Europe during the first three-quarters of the nineteenth century.

[1] *Works of Sir William Jones,* edited by Lord Teignmouth, 1804, vol. ii, p. 268. The italics are Sir William Jones's.

In 1808 Friedrich Schlegel (1772–1829) published his book on *The Language and Wisdom of the Indians,* in which he carried out in detail the comparison between Sanskrit and the European languages suggested by Jones in his address of 1786. By tracing the similarities in vocabulary and grammatical structure, he established beyond any doubt the family relationship between Sanskrit and the better-known languages of Europe, chiefly Greek, Latin, and German. He is the first, so far as I know, to use the phrase "comparative grammar."

Rasmus Rask (1787–1832), the Danish scholar, by his genius for linguistic studies, by his comprehensive first-hand knowledge of many languages obtained by extensive travels from Sweden to India (1816–23), and by his method of painstaking comparison and classification of languages on the basis of grammatical structure, and of similarity and difference in the most essential and indispensable words, became in a very true sense the actual founder of the modern science of language.

Jakob Grimm (1785–1863)—with the co-operation of his brother Wilhelm (1786–1859)—was first led to the investigation of language through his study of old German popular poetry and folklore. Starting with Rask's observation of certain regular "consonant shifts" in the transition of certain groups of words from Greek and Latin into the Germanic languages, he formulated what is now known as "Grimm's

Law," which revealed certain hitherto unnoticed consonant relations between well-known words in these
two groups of languages, and in this way gave a new
fascination and impulse to the science of comparative
philology, which has continued from the publication
of Grimm's comparative *German Grammar* in 1822
down to the present time. He was also the first philologist to separate language from literature, and to
raise all languages, and even dialects, to a common
level of dignity for purposes of scientific study, independent of the value of the literature which they
might or might not possess.

Franz Bopp (1791–1867), the next significant con-
tributor to linguistic science, received his first impulse
towards comparative language study from Schlegel's
book referred to above, on *The Language and Wisdom of the Indians,* which was published, as we have
noticed, in 1808 while Bopp was still a student of
seventeen at the Lyceum in Bavaria. In 1812 he went
to Paris at the expense of the Bavarian Government
to study Sanskrit. After four years' study there he
published in 1816—when he was twenty-five—his
first and most important book, *On the Conjugation
System of the Sanskrit Language in Comparison with
Greek, Latin, Persian, and German.* Schlegel and his
followers had already established the family relationship among these languages. Bopp was inspired with
the hope that by a complete analytic comparison of
the grammars of these related languages he could dis-

cover their oldest recorded shapes, and by this route
might be able to discover the ultimate origin of grammatical forms. The preliminary work of comparison
was so well done that while he failed in his quest for
the ultimate origin of language, he founded the
science of Comparative Grammar—"à peu près
comme Christophe Colomb a découvert l'Amérique
en cherchant la route des Indes (Meillet). In recognition of this fact, the Bopp Foundation, for the pro-
motion of the study of Sanskrit and Comparative
Grammar, was established at Berlin in 1866, the
fiftieth anniversary of the publication of his book, by
contributions from scholars in all parts of the world.
Bopp was appointed professor of Sanskrit and Comparative Grammar at Berlin in 1822, and continued
writing and publishing there on comparative languages until his death in 1867.

Wilhelm von Humboldt (1767–1835) was not so
much a philologist as a philosopher who chose language as the chief object of his philosophical investigations. He developed the theory that the structure of
each separate language grew out of and reflected the
peculiar mental life of the people who made it, and
that each language had therefore its own individuality which separated it from all other languages. The
essay in which he presented this view, *The Hetero-
geneity of Language and Its Influence upon the Intellectual Development of Mankind*—published in
1836, the year after his death—has often been called

"the text-book of the philosophy of speech," a tribute to the force with which he developed his thesis. His insistence upon essential differences between languages is pertinent here, since the object of the present treatise is to establish the opposite point of view, namely, first, the identity of the problem which originally called language into existence in all parts of the world, and, second, the consequent identity of the basic structure of all languages in meeting this problem, despite the individual differences that have entered into the various languages made by various races of people.

The names given above mark sufficiently for our purpose the steps in the development of language science and theory from Herder to the middle of the nineteenth century. Two more names must be added to bring us from that point to the eighteen-seventies when Darwin entered the field.

Max Müller (1823–1900,) the German-English philologist and philosopher, and William Dwight Whitney (1827–94), the American philologist, came at a time—they did the important part of their language work between 1850 and 1875—when the young science of language had already made sufficient progress to claim a place of respect among the other modern sciences. Their work consisted mainly in gathering together, sifting, and unifying into some kind of single view the best of the work that had been done in the preceding seventy-odd years. Both of them had, though in quite different ways, "the gift of expression," which enabled them to present their views in a style which was scientifically adequate and at the same time popular, and which rendered a high service to the science of language by bringing it out of the enclosed field of specialists and making it understandable and attractive to the general reader who had an interest in human history and development. In this respect they did for linguistics, though in a lesser way, what Darwin in the corresponding years did for biology.

Max Müller was born and educated in Germany. After graduating from Leipzig he went to Berlin University, where he learned comparative philology from Bopp, and philosophy from Schelling. He came to Oxford in 1850, and lived, lectured, and wrote there until his death in 1900. His chief strength as a philologist was his imaginative insight. He saw the living significance of words, which gave him a clue to their relations and life-history, and guided him in selecting and arranging them into a system. In this way he did much towards transforming the growing mass of language material from a mere burden of the memory to a significant structure of the reason, whose various parts suggested and sustained each other easily in the mind; and incidentally he raised the status of his reader from hod-carrier to architect, whose interest was not merely in carrying loads of word-material at a master's bidding, but in the actual reconstruction of the word-edifice which told the story of human progress. His aim in philology was similar to Darwin's in biology, but the field was more subtle and recondite, much of the necessary factual material was lost or obscured by time, and more pertinent still, Müller had not the same comprehensive synthetic grasp of the whole field as Darwin had, so that his work had nothing like the rounded completeness of Darwin's which renders it capable of being easily held and visualized in a single view.

Müller's gift of style, of figure, and rhetoric, which was very similar to Huxley's in science, gave imaginative concreteness to his work, frequently raising his science into literature. But his strength here was at times his weakness. Fascinated by the symmetry of the structure he was building, he had a tendency to strain or modify the facts so as to make it fit more neatly its particular niche in the system. His impulse towards rhetoric often led him also into colourful and telling forms of expression where the subject required quietness and precision.

Another impulse also tended to lead Max Müller astray in his theory of language. He seemed to be obsessed with the desire to win for linguistics a place of respect and dignity equal to that already accorded the older and better-established natural sciences. Hence in the opening chapter of his first important book, *The Science of Language* (1861), he writes: "I always took it for granted that the science of language, which is best known in this country by the name of comparative philology, is one of the physical sciences, and that therefore its method ought to be the same as that which has been followed with so much success in botany, geology, anatomy, and other branches of the study of nature." This physical-science bias led him to his peculiar cause-and-effect theory of the origin of language. In nature, he says, every object when struck by a solid body responds with its own peculiar sound. Hence the four hundred-odd original roots of language, which the philologists at that time thought they had discovered, were, according to Müller's physical theory, the original "phonetic types or typical sounds" which man's mind gave off in response to the various impacts which the world made upon it.[1] "What is antecedent to the production of these roots is the work of nature; what follows after is the work of man." [2] Just how or why

---

[1] It may be interesting to notice that Mr. J. B. Watson's most recent exposition of language (*Behaviorism,* revised edition, 1930, Chap. X), apart from its new behaviourist diction and phraseology, is a logical development of Max Müller's theory here. All human behaviour of action, thought, and speech is explained by Mr. Watson as phases of the simple formula of "stimulus and response." "The behaviorist," he says, "advances a natural theory about thinking which makes it just as simple, and just as much a part of biological processes, as tennis playing" (p. 238). Speech is thinking "aloud in words" (p. 246), and "speaking overtly or to ourselves (thinking) is just as objective a type of behavior as baseball" (p. 6). Thought and language are both explained as the materials of an objective natural science. After a careful reading, however, of Mr. Watson's interesting exposition of thought and language by reducing them to simple phases of "stimulus and response," one has the uneasy feeling that he is being induced, to borrow an apt phrase from the late Professor J. S. Haldane, "to take a gigantic leap in the dark."

[2] Max Müller, *Collected Works,* vol. i, p. 533.

the first part of the history of language should be considered as the work of nature and the second part as
the work of man is not very clear. Fortunately he did
not consistently hold to his physical-science theory
of language. Most of his work, and by far the most
valuable part of it, is concerned with language development as a non-physical phenomenon.

He had an extensive and, in most cases, an exact
knowledge of words and languages, and one is constantly surprised at the many vital suggestions which
are found in his works. He popularized the science
enormously and stirred his students to an enthusiasm
corresponding to his own. One cannot read his books
without being curiously stimulated by them, even if
the stimulus is often, as it was to his American contemporary philologist, Whitney, one of antipathy;
and like some of Ruskin's art criticisms, by his genius
for making dead things live, his errors are often more
valuable than true findings of pedantic scholars.

Max Müller's contemporary and co-worker in the
task of giving a unified view of linguistic science as
it stood in the third quarter of the nineteenth century
was the American philologist, W. D. Whitney. Curiously enough, both scholars were trained under the
same teacher. After two years' study of Sanskrit at
Yale University, Whitney went to Berlin—in the
same year, 1850, in which Müller left Berlin for
Oxford—to take a three years' course in Sanskrit
under Bopp. On his return to America in 1854 he was

appointed professor of Sanskrit at Yale, where he lived and worked until his death in 1894, the hundredth anniversary of the death of Sir William Jones, "the founder of Indo-European philology." Incidentally Whitney was the winner of the first Bopp prize awarded by the Berlin Academy of Science in 1870 "for the most important contribution to Sanskrit philology during the preceding three years."

The two books in which Whitney gave his summarized view of linguistic science, with significant contributions of his own, *Language and the Study of Language* (1867) and *The Life and Growth of Language* (1875), were translated into several languages, and were hardly less popular than those of his co-worker and antagonist in the field, Max Müller. The second book covers with some important modifications the same ground as the first, and the fact that it was designed to give, as the author says, "an outline of linguistic science," based upon "the now generally accepted facts of language," and that it was written at the request of the publishers of the International Scientific Series (it appeared as vol. xvi of the series), indicates that the young science of language had won its place among the older sciences. Though nominally an "outline" of the science of language up to that time, the book when finished, by the clear organization of the already available material and theories, and by its numerous original and fruitful suggestions, proved itself to be a distinct contribu-

tion to the new science. His discussion of "The
Nature and Origin of Language" (Chap. XIV) is as
valuable and valid as anything written before or
since, and is still, on the whole, perhaps the best single
chapter available on that subject. His differentiation
between human language and the cries of animals is
unusually precise and clear, and is in most points convincing still, despite the bias which Darwin and his
disciples have given to the thinking on that question.

The preceding paragraphs bring us to the close of
the third quarter of the nineteenth century, a hundred years from Herder's essay. During this period
the question of the beginnings and development of
language, while discussed in a purely scientific and
philosophical manner, was confined to the human
species alone, in the belief that the capacity for language was unique in man, and separated him from
the animal world beneath him. Max Müller and
Whitney, the chief representatives of the linguistic
thought of the time, both clearly stated the position,
and a sentence from each will give the definite starting point for the next stage of our advance. "What,
then," Müller asks, "is the difference between brute
and man? What is it that man can do, and of which
we find no signs, no rudiments, in the whole brute
world? I answer without hesitation: the one great
barrier between the brute and man is Language"
(*Science of Language, Collected Works,* vol. ii, p.
489). "But, as things are," Whitney writes, "every

community of men has a common language, while none of the lower animals are possessed of such; their means of communication being of so different a character that it has no right to be called by the same name" (*Life and Growth of Language,* Chap. XIV, p. 281, 1875).[1] These two quotations give quite adequately the view, regarding man and language, which was held by linguistic scientists from 1772, when Herder first clearly formulated it in his essay, until Darwin entered the field in 1871.

[1] One may be excused for calling attention here to a characteristic difference in these two sentences. The dogmatic certainty and emphatic pointedness of Müller's statement, and the unemphatic, careful, measured quietness of Whitney's are like differentiating portraits of the two minds and their manner of working. One has more confidence in the writer whose "yea is yea, and nay, nay; for whatsoever is more than this cometh of evil."

CHAPTER VI

DARWIN

In this year falls the fiftieth anniversary of the death of Charles Darwin—one of those rare individuals who have altered the main trend of thought and inaugurated a new attitude and a new outlook in human affairs.—JULIAN HUXLEY, *Contemporary Review*, October 1932.

Language has justly been considered as one of the chief distinctions between man and the lower animals. But man, as a highly competent judge, Archbishop Whately, remarks, "is not the only animal that can make use of language to express what is passing in his mind, and can understand, more or less, what is so expressed by another."—DARWIN, *Descent of Man*, Chap. III.

❖   ❖   ❖   ❖

1. *Darwin's Expansion of the Problem*

THE INVESTIGATION OF LANGUAGE, AS POINTED OUT in the last chapter, had been carried on for a hundred years in the belief that language was a unique characteristic of man, and did not extend to the animal world beneath him. But with the publication of the *Descent of Man* in 1871 the whole problem of language was suddenly expanded into a much wider region. Darwin, in that book, distinctly challenged the human boundaries that had been set to language

95

as being artificial and arbitrary, and extended the problem over into the animal world, maintaining that the difference between the language of man and the cries of animals was not a difference in kind, as had been formerly thought, but a difference in degree only, a difference in definiteness of connotation and distinctness of articulation. This difference in language followed naturally, he maintained, upon the difference in degree of their mental development.

Max Müller, with other philologists, opposed Darwin's view, claiming that articulate language was the evidence of man's "power of abstraction," a power which differentiated him completely from the animals. Darwin and his scientific colleagues replied that animals had also this power of abstraction, and produced a considerable body of evidence from the mental habits of animals (Chaps. III and IV in the *Descent of Man*), which was at least plausible enough to win the majority of votes from the semi-scientific reading public before whom the debate was carried on.

Meantime neither party gave any exact definition of the word *abstraction,* upon which the controversy turned; nor did either party give any sufficiently accurate definition of the *articulate language* of man that would enable them to come to a precise answer as to whether it was the same as or different from the so-called language of the animals. And so, as often happens in heated debate, the meanings of the two significant words, *abstraction* and *articulate language,* which occupied the centre of the controversy, remained themselves involved in a mist, which prevented any kind of precise comparison between the language of man and the cries of animals.

Before the end of the nineteenth century, however, the Darwinian theory of evolution in general, together with the subsidiary theory of the identification of man and the lower animals with respect to both their intelligence and their language, had so completely won its way, both with the scientists themselves and with the general reading public, that the other side of the argument had sunk almost entirely out of view. It has hardly shown its head since. It is customary now and a mark of modernism to speak of the language of animals and the language of man as merely two branches of the same thing, as though there were no longer any doubt about the question. One purpose of the present treatment is to open the question again and to re-examine more closely the difference between man and the animals which Darwin practically obliterated some sixty-six years ago; to discover if possible what specifically happened when man emerged from animal nature into a new world, whose new conditions necessitated articulate language. What were the limits of the animal world from which he emerged whose needs were answered by a few natural cries; what were the new horizons, new needs, new potentialities opened to him in his new world whose actualization urged him to the making of language?

2. *Darwin's Contribution to the Investigation*

> On her great venture, Man,
> Earth gazes while her fingers dint the breast
> Which is his well of strength, his home of rest,
> And fair to scan.
> GEORGE MEREDITH, *Earth and Man.*

Before undertaking a criticism of Darwin's arguments with a view to answering the questions raised at the close of the preceding chapter, one should say a word or two upon the positive contribution which Darwin has made to the whole question. He advanced the investigation of the problem of language definitely, as it seems to me, in three ways.

First. Previous to the appearance of Darwin's book it had always been assumed that the problem of language was confined to the life of man; that it was a product of man's reason, and that man's reason marked him off distinctly from the rest of the world. Darwin distinctly challenged this view, maintaining that man is not separated from the animal world, either by his intelligence or his language, except in degree of development. He presented this new view with such force, and supported it with so much concrete evidence, that the old view of man's unique position in the world could never again be merely assumed or taken for granted. If man *does* occupy a unique position, that position must now be described and made explicitly clear. So that whether Darwin was right or wrong he unequivocally raised the problem into view, so as to give a very definite starting point for any new advance in the steps towards its solution.

Second. Darwin brought together so large a body of facts, and pointed out so many characteristics of animal life which rises in ascending steps towards the life of man, that we have now a very completely detailed picture of the whole background of nature out of which the life of man emerges; so that if man has actually risen to, and does actually hold, a unique and solitary position in the known world, the background of animal nature beneath him is now so fully elaborated that man's characteristic portrait may be distinctly drawn in comparison and contrast with it.

Third. Darwin's work has brought home to our minds in a most distinct way the view that man is a natural and integral part of the world, and not a mere exotic, or foreigner, or temporary sojourner placed by deliberate external design upon the surface of an alien world of mechanical forces which are externally manipulated in his exclusive interests. That is his third contribution to our better understanding of the world.

On this last point, however, it is worth while noting that not very many modern scientists or modern readers and writers in general have come to a full realization of what Darwin has done in this last respect. Darwin himself seems never to have absorbed this idea of the organic unity of the world from matter to man so completely into his mind as to fix it there as a permanent and native element in his instinctive thought and speech. To the end, at least when off his guard, he continued to speak of man *and* the world as two separate though related things rather than as two phases of the one thing. This was, no doubt, due, in part at least, to the rigidity of language and its consequent limitations for the immediate expression of a new idea. But it was due also to the difficulty of assimilating and domesticating a new and radical idea within the mind so that it will function unconsciously there in adjusting one's instinctive thought and speech to the new view.[1]

Most modern scientists continue to speak of the material world of mechanical forces as the real and permanent world, and of man with all his mental faculties and moral purposes as an extrinsic chance-comer and would-be usurper, that by some kind of "biological accident," as Mr. Santayana puts it, has got upon the surface of a physical world of mechanical forces that have no intrinsic connection with the higher part of his own life, his mental and moral aims. This pseudo-scientific view appears in various

---

[1] Since making the first draft of this paragraph I have been struck by Mr. Bernard Shaw's determined statement of the unity or identity of man and the world in *Man and Superman,* Act III, p. 133.

ways in much of the representative poetry and fiction
of the last seventy-five years, as well as in science and
philosophy. Matthew Arnold's statement of man's relation to the world he lives in in *Empedocles*:

> No, we are strangers here; the world is from of old,

or

> To tunes we did not call our being must keep chime,

are typical examples of it; and Arnold, like some of
the materialistic scientists for whom he speaks, takes
some pride in thus facing "unpalatable facts," and
stating them frankly. In Thomas Hardy's representation of life and the world in his greatest novels, as
The Return of the Native or *Tess of the d'Urbervilles,*
and in many of his metaphysical poems, the deter-
mining agencies of the world, mechanical for the
most part, and always blind and powerful, are conceived as not merely indifferent to man's destiny, but
often as in an actually sinister relation to it.

This dualism between man's higher destiny and the
world out of which he emerged is not in consonance
with the aim and tenor of Darwin's work, even
though Darwin himself did not, as I think, succeed in
developing his view into a concrete logical philosophy. He did believe in the organic unity of the world
from matter to man, and in his books, especially the
Origin and the *Descent,* he has amassed and organized such a body of evidence upon the resemblances between man and the animals with respect

both to their physical and mental qualities, and between the animals and the lower forms of life, that we can hardly ever again think of man as separate from the world. The whole world now appears to us as a single world; and if this view is right, then man with his complex physiological structure, and all his mental faculties and moral purposes as well, has in some way or other come out of this same world, and has risen by gradual steps, many of which still lie hidden, into the position where he now stands. Darwin, as pointed out above, was not the originator of this organic view of the world, but accepting the general view from his predecessors and contemporaries, he assembled and organized such a mass of concrete evidence in support of it, and presented it in such a popular, readable, and logical form as to give the organic view of the world an almost universal currency among thinking readers. In this respect his was without doubt the most distinct contribution of the last seventy-five years to our better understanding of the world.

3. *Darwin's Argument*

> Why language, then, to man confined?
> The dog can say what 's in his mind.
> > *Odd Rhymes.*

Darwin, though convinced of the organic unity of the world in its evolution from its lowest to its highest forms, did not succeed in completely establishing his conviction by logical proof or actual evidence. There were at least two gaps in the development process that he saw no way of bridging: (*a*) the gap between inorganic and organic nature, and (*b*) the gap between organic nature without intelligence and organic nature with intelligence. In the third chapter of the *Descent* he writes: "In what manner the mental powers were first developed in the lowest organisms is as hopeless an inquiry as how life itself first originated. These are problems for the distant future, if they are ever to be solved by man." Scientists since Darwin's time, who believe with him that life and mind were not always co-present with matter in world history, but emerged at some given time from lifeless and mindless ancestry, have from time to time given attention to the first of these two problems, namely the connection between non-living and living matter, but have as yet made no measurable advance from Darwin's position. Mr. Lloyd Morgan, speaking as a biologist in his latest book, *Emergence of Novelty* (1933), writes: "Of the passage from matter to life, if it occurred as an original novelty, along a suite of emergent steps, we are as yet wholly in the region of evolutionary conjecture."

But a third gap that was always thought to exist, Darwin, as noted above, did attempt to close, and, as far as the minds of what is called the intelligent public were concerned, succeeded in closing, at least for the last twenty-five years; the gap, namely, between the intelligence of the animals and the intelligence of man. Having successfully established the general evolutionary theory within the plant and animal life of the world in the *Origin of Species,* he was then confronted with the further question: "In what relation does man stand to the rest of the animal life of the world?" This is the question which he answers in the *Descent of Man,* 1871, and the significant parts of that book are the third and fourth chapters, where he makes the "Comparison of the Mental Powers of Man and the Lower Animals." He puts his view and purpose quite clearly in the opening lines of the third chapter. "My object in this chapter," he says, "is to show that there is no fundamental difference between man and the higher mammals in their mental faculties." Recognizing that language is connected with the mental faculties, Darwin includes his now well-known discussion of language in the closing part of the same third chapter. He opens the discussion with the following: "The faculty of language has justly been considered as one of the chief distinctions between man and the lower animals. But man, as a highly competent judge, Archbishop Whately, remarks, is not the only animal that can make use of language to express what is passing in his mind, and can understand more or less what is expressed by another. . . . In Paraguay the *Cebus Azarae* when excited utters at least six distinct sounds, which excite in other monkeys similar emotions." The dog barks "in at least four or five distinct sounds." From accumulated evidence of this kind Darwin draws the conclusion at the end of the fourth chapter, to use his own words, that "the difference in mind between man and the higher animals, great as it is, certainly is one of degree and not of kind." The same he holds to be true of language.

Throughout these two chapters Darwin supports his view of the identity of the various mental faculties of man with those of the lower animals, and of the identity of their languages, by the evidence of facts which he has either observed himself or has received from other trustworthy observers. The facts which he presents in order to show that animals possess the various mental faculties and emotions which he ascribes to them, and language as well—in *his* connotation of language—would, I think, be accepted by every unprejudiced reader, except the facts and evidence submitted in his paragraph on the imagination. This exception turns out to be a very vital one, and we shall return to it later.

4. *The Evidence from Language against Darwin's View*

On the whole, man's development and control over language is unquestionably the greatest single achievement which his intelligence has compassed, and whether one thinks of it as cause or effect, its presence, more than any other one factor, is responsible for his enormous superiority to his animal neighbours.—*The Evolution of Intelligence,* J. R. ANGELL, President of Yale University.

Meantime there is one large body of facts that stands in contradiction to Darwin's whole case. The animals and birds of nature have each, as he points out, a certain number of natural sounds—not the conventionalized sounds of language—say from one to twelve, that have significance for others of their kind; and these sounds, he maintains, must be called language, because they do not differ from the language of man except in degree of distinctness. Ancestral man, if our theory of natural evolution is true, had also in his early natural life a certain number of natural sounds, say twelve, that had significance for his own kind, and perhaps for other animals about him. Now, there are two things to be noted in these natural sounds as we find them among the animals and birds of to-day, and as we assume they were with preconscious man, two things which distinguish them from language.

First, they are *natural* sounds, and consequently *indefinite* in significance. They are like the few mere exclamations or cries of pleasure or pain which man still uses and which convey to the hearer no *definite* significance, either of the kind of pain or of the specific cause of it. We call these cries interjections, i.e. unconventionalized sounds *interjected* into the structure of language proper. They are somewhat analogous to the sounds of instrumental music which affect the mind of the hearer only in a vague and undefined way.

Second, the animals do not increase the number of their few natural sounds, nor do they show any impulse or tendency or need to increase them as time goes on, except where man deliberately interferes in order to effect a temporary increase in the imitative vocabulary, say, of the parrot. The few instinctive natural sounds without increase seem to satisfy the needs and capacity of the animal's mind, and to correspond with its nature.

These two things bring us to the point of difference between man and the animals with respect to language. At some time and, as it seems to me, from some creative and purposive force at work in the world, there emerged into life within the mind of man a new power or faculty for *explicitly* differentiating the objects of the world, both in their distribution in space and their succession in time; and with this awakened power of explicit differentiation a consequent need and corresponding impulse for something far more definite and elaborate than the few nebulous or misty-edged natural sounds which satisfied his preconscious needs. And eventually with this new power of explicit differentiation, and his urge to actualize it, man got started upon a free course, first, of shaping these vague natural sounds into definite-edged or definitely articulated sounds—words, as we now call them—

that could be clearly distinguished from one another; and second, of investing each definite sound with a definite meaning, a conventional and arbitrary meaning as distinguished from the vague natural significance of natural sounds; and third, of increasing or multiplying without limit the number of these definitely shaped conventionalized sounds. By these three things, the definite shaping of natural sounds, the conventionalization of their meaning, and their multiplication without limit, man has elaborated out of his few original sounds an immense structure of articulate language whose parts are as distinctly differentiated and organized as are the objects of the natural world which this language fabric now reflects. The two conventionalized sounds "dog" and "cat," for example, are as clearly differentiated from one another as are the two natural objects for which they stand. Meantime, the animal world lies unawakened at man's feet without, as we said, showing any need, impulse, or power for transmuting their natural cries into articulate sounds, investing them with conventional meanings, or increasing their number.

This is an enormous difference between man and the animals, a difference in actualized fact not in theory, too obvious to be questioned when attention is called to it, and too significant to be overlooked; and it stands, as I have said, in unequivocal contradiction to the whole tenor of Darwin's arguments. It is true, as remarked above, that certain birds under man's instruction can be taught, by some kind of instinctive imitation of both sound and content, to increase the number of their own natural sounds; but they show no power of breaking through the "charmed circle of nature," in which they are in some way confined, into the realm of *free and conscious mind* where articulate language has its birth and growth, and in which man now "lives, moves, and has his being."

Now this shaping and conventionalization of natural sounds, giving to each a definite form and specific connotation, and the consequent free, unlimited cumulative development of human language as contrasted with the few, fixed, stationary, uncumulative natural cries of animals must be due to some very real difference in their respective mental powers. To say that this difference is merely a difference in "degree" and not in "kind" of intelligence at this stage of the inquiry tells us nothing. Man has broken through some barrier which, up to the present time at least, encloses the minds of the animals, and the plain scientific question confronting us now is: "What *is* the difference between the two?"

5. *"Kind" and "Degree"*

To clear the way toward an exact answer to this question a word should be said first upon the diction to be used. There is no longer any profit to be gained by dwelling upon the question which Darwin took as the starting point and pivot of his discussion sixty-six years ago, the question whether this difference between animals and man is one of *kind* or *degree*. The two words, as already noted, were never clearly defined or differentiated, although at that time they did stand, in a general way, for two different points of view, two opposing schools of thought, and Darwin's use of them was perhaps the most effective method for breaking down the traditional dualistic view, and removing the prejudice that stood in the way of a free scientific consideration of the whole question. But now that the prejudice is gone, the original need of the two words in their general significance has disappeared, and they have no sufficiently precise significance that would render them useful at the present advanced stage of the inquiry. What we now need is an exact and concrete marking of specific likenesses and differences, and these two long-bandied-about words are no longer accurate enough for that purpose. The vagueness of their connotation, overlooked in their former general use, becomes apparent as soon as one attempts to use them with precision, so that they cloud the issue instead of clearing it. To reassure myself on this point I recently asked a well-known biologist if he could give me from the whole field of biology one clear example of a difference which scientists would unequivocally agree upon as a difference in kind, and another which they would agree upon as a difference in degree, so that there would be no longer any doubt about the precise meanings of the two words. He was unable to give the required examples. I have since put the query to a number of other scientists and psychologists with no better luck.

This alone makes it clear that to get forward now in the investigation we must discard these two misty words. And since the organic unity of the world including man—thanks chiefly to Darwin—seems to be now pretty generally accepted, we might assume all differences to be differences of degree only; and assuming this, we may profitably discard both words and speak simply of differences, differences in the explicit forms of life and mind which have successively emerged in the spiral course of evolutionary advance.

Some of these differences, however, and among them, as I shall try to show, the difference in mental power between man and the animals, are vital and significant; and although misconceived as totally disparate realms in pre-Darwin times, their legitimate boundaries have been blurred during the last sixty years through the pressure for unity by Darwin and the neo-Darwinians. But now that the pressure is relaxed by the lapse of time and the disappearance of opposition, these differences are emerging into notice again, and the time has come in our thinking when their characteristic differences must be analysed and described closely and concretely, and their signifi-

cance specially marked in relation to one another and
to the general underlying unity. For this closer work,
general categories like "kind" and "degree" can render no service. A more precise diction is required.

Realizing then the difference described above between the large and rapidly growing structure of the
articulate language of man, and the meagre static
body of the natural sounds of animals, we are confronted with the plain concrete question: What *is*
this difference in mental power that has enabled man
to so "get the start" of the *natural* world and "bear
the palm alone"? Is the difference of such a kind as
can be concretely analysed and described so as to set
out the significant characteristics of the human mind
in clear and definite differentiation from the background of animal intelligence?

I think it can be so described, and if one can succeed in doing this one should be able to come fairly
upon the origin of language, and its nature as a phenomenon in the world; for language, as I think can
be shown, arose just out of this difference, arose in
answer to the new mental problem that confronted
man when he emerged from the realm of animal
nature into the realm of free mind.

6. *The Fallacy in Darwin's Method*

I—this thought which is called I—is the mould into
which the world is poured like melted wax.—EMERSON, *The
Transcendentalist,* 1842.

Why, it may be asked, in the investigation of language origin, should one go back to Darwin when so much has been written since both on evolution and on language? The answer is that Darwin's name still stands at the centre of the modern point of view, and while his views on language in 1871 have not altered to any extent the progress of the specific science of language since that time, they have altered in a very significant way our philosophy or general conception of language in relation to other phenomena in the world. They have, as a matter of fact, from the date of their publication deflected the philosophy of language from the natural course which it had been following for the previous hundred years, and the first step now in any new investigation is to correct if possible that deflection.

In the *Descent of Man,* as noted above, Darwin undertook to complete the story which was begun in the *Origin of Species* by making the final connecting link between the animal intelligence and the intelligence of man, thus establishing his theory of the complete organic unity of the world. But, as also pointed out above, in his intuitive and right sense of organic unity, and in his strong desire to establish it by logical proof, he overlooked, and for the time obliterated, the cardinal difference between the two. His oversight and obscuration of this difference was due to a lurking fallacy and a consequent fundamental error in his method of comparison.

The error was summarily this: Throughout the discussion he makes no inquiry into the nature of the total or *central* unifying mental faculty of man, nor of the corresponding *central* unifying mental faculty of the animals; nor does he make any comparison between these two. He proceeds by enumerating the separate sub-faculties, instincts, and emotions, which psychology has differentiated within the total faculty of reason, and taking these one by one he finds by comparison that the animal seems to possess them all in at least an incipient degree. He finds, for example, that the animals have the same senses as man, the same instincts, the same emotions, such as fear, terror, suspicion, courage, timidity, rage, revenge, as well as the more complex emotions of jealousy, shame, modesty, scorn, humour; that they possess also the more intellectual emotions, such as wonder and curiosity; and that they show the same powers of imitation, attention, memory, imagination, and reason. Finding no apparent difference in the operation of these differentiated sub-faculties in animals and in man, he merely adds up the results instead of unifying them; and comes to the quite illegitimate conclusion that there is no difference in the *total faculty* of reason in each; no difference between the central unifying mental faculty of animals and the corresponding mental faculty of man—the *nous,* as Aristotle calls it in his *Posterior Analytics*—which coordinates and uses as its agents the differentiated sub-faculties, and which, in man, is conscious both of itself and its sub-faculties, and can examine and carry on a discussion about them as we are doing here. He moves forward in such a plain manner and with such clear matter-of-fact evidence, that the reader is seduced into the same logical error.

But this method of reasoning and deduction is clearly not sound. We cannot pass at a jump from the apparent identity of these differentiated sub-faculties in man and the lower animals, to the identity of the central faculty of reason itself, which, as we have pointed out, includes and uses as its instruments all these subordinate faculties. And the significant difference between man and the animals, which opened the way to articulate language for man, while restricting animals to natural cries, seems to be a difference in the central unifying faculty, and not in its subordinate agents. For this reason the new investigation which follows here will consist in a comparison of the unified faculty of mind in man and the animals respectively, with a view to discovering the difference between the two which led man to articulate language and left the animals without it.

SECTION II

The New Investigation

INTRODUCTION
THE PROBLEM

We must therefore see the whole varied congeries of living things as a single very ancient Being, of inconceivable vastness, and animated by one Spirit.—SAMUEL BUTLER, *God the Known and God the Unknown.*

Science has opened all kinds of perspectives. In particular it has shown life as a slow upward-evolving process. It has shown that there is something in evolution which we must call progress, and it has shown that we ourselves are now trustees for any evolutionary progress that remains to be made.—JULIAN HUXLEY, *Science and Social Needs,* 1936.

WHAT, THEN, IS THE DIFFERENCE BETWEEN THE central unifying faculty of reason in man, out of which language arose, and the corresponding central faculty in the animals, which expresses itself in a few natural cries; and how in our present state of knowledge can this difference be distinctly brought into

117

view and described in a concrete way? This is a complex question, and can be best answered for our purpose by breaking it into four parts.

First. What was the actual nature of the world of matter, and of plant and animal life, before the awakening of conscious reason in man?

Second. What were the nature and characteristics of the new mental power that then came to life and actuality in man?

Third. What new problem came into existence with the emergence of this new mental power, that gave birth to the articulate and cumulative language of man?

Fourth. What was the predestined form and structure of language to meet this new problem of free and conscious mind

I shall attempt a plain, concrete descriptive answer to these four questions in order.

CHAPTER I

THE PRE-CONSCIOUS WORLD:
A SPACE-AND-TIME PICTURE

But deepest of all illusory Appearances are your two
grand world-enveloping Appearances, Space and Time.
—CARLYLE, *Sartor Resartus*, 1830.

The Prime, that willed ere wareness was,
Whose Brain perchance is Space, whose Thought its laws.
THOMAS HARDY, *The Dynasts.*

❖   ❖   ❖   ❖

1. *The Space-Picture*

QUESTION ONE. WHAT WERE THE NATURE AND
characteristics of the world in its three main divisions
of matter, plant life, and animal life, before it
emerged to its fourth main division in the explicitly
conscious life of man? The answer to this question
carries us backward in time to a period so remote
from the present that no answer would be at all possible were it not that in his emergence to consciousness man rose above the time-stream of sense, and by
the help of language has been able to recover and
reconstruct the otherwise irrecoverable past. While
the actual sense-facts which constituted the natural
environment contemporary with man's emergence
have long since vanished in the stream of change, we

know now, from our knowledge of the past and present, that in any piece of virgin timber or park land of to-day we should have, substantially and typically, the same natural environment from which man emerged thousands of years ago. We should have, first of all, the same inorganic world of fixed geographic relations and definite structures: sun, moon, stars, clouds, winds, waters, soil, rocks, etc.; second, the differentiated forms of organic insentient life: grass, flowers, shrubs, trees, etc.; third, the various forms of sentient life: fishes, birds, reptiles, mammals; all these multitudinous forms, inorganic and organic, differentiated from each other and united with each other in a complete network of space, time, and causal relations. That, in epitome, is a space-picture of the world of nature as it confronts our eyes to-day, and the only significant animal absent from it, that we would have found in the old pre-conscious world, is the natural animallike progenitor of man. In his *actualized* life, however, at that period—if our evolutionary theory is the true one—he would be only one more animal whose actual presence, if we omit his potential destiny, would not alter the significant characteristics of the general picture.

2. *The Time-Picture*

Modern science and philosophy, however, have discovered that this contemporary space-picture has a history; that its present complex and highly differentiated features are the product of a time-evolution; and science and philosophy have also succeeded in recovering and reconstructing in its main outlines that past time-picture of the world which we require as the complement and interpretation of the contemporary space-picture. By drawing the outlines of this time-picture, and noting the significant differences that came into explicit existence as the developing force at work in the world emerged from inorganic to organic insentient life in the vegetable world, and again from insentient to sentient life in the animal world, we shall be able to see more distinctly the significant characteristics that came to life and actuality in the last step from inconscious sentient to conscious sentient life, i.e. man. To outline this time-picture and mark as we go the significant emerging differences will be our next step, and, at the risk of appearing elementary, I shall do this very simply and with considerable detail.

Furthermore, I shall construct the picture on the hypothesis of the complete organic unity of the world from matter to man. I assume, in other words, that man in his complete life, his mental powers and his moral purposes, no less than in his physical organism, is a natural product and a natural part of the world; and that in the general evolution of the matter-life-and-mind of the world man eventually emerged from some original diffused or permeating life-and-mind force into an actual, individualized, objective organism and explicitly purposive agent as we now find him. To regard man's physical organism as having come out of the world by natural evolution, and his mental powers and moral aims as having come in some accidental way from other than natural sources, is a dualism of modern mechanistic thought which seems as naïve from a philosophic point of view as any of the older superstitions which it has replaced. If the world is in verity the organic unity which we claim it to be, then man is not merely *in* the world or *on* it. He *is* the world at the highest point of its physico-mental life that we know on this planet; and the specific purpose of the present treatise is to differentiate this last phase of the world, that has emerged to actuality in the body and mind of man, from its next lower phase in animal life.

A large part of the contemporary space-picture outlined in the preceding section is made up of distinctly differentiated organic forms of both insentient and sentient life. But there was a period in the time-picture of the world, if we can trust our science, when none of these differentiated organic forms were to be found in actualized existence upon the earth's surface; a time when only those forms or formations which we now call inorganic could be found in actual existence there. If a company of modern scientists could at that period have stepped upon this globe with their fully equipped modern laboratories they might have given an adequate explanation of all they found by means of the physical sciences alone, mathematics, physics, chemistry, geology, etc. It would be a material world organized in the media of space and time, and explained by the mechanical law of "matter, motion, and force." That the earth had a long pre-organic history, a long evolution of changing and developing inorganic formations before the concrete living forms emerged upon its surface, seems now to be reasonably certain. What the specific nature or duration of this pre-organic history may have been does not materially affect our present purpose.

Our interest begins with the emergence of life, and here we are met with a problem that is still unsolved. "How life itself first originated" was, in Darwin's estimate in 1871, a "hopeless inquiry," "a problem for the distant future if it is ever to be solved by man." Mr. Lloyd Morgan writes in 1926: "There is as yet no plain tale of the passage from the non-living to the living" (*Life, Mind and Spirit*, p. 77). The problem is still in the dark as far as specific or scientific knowledge of it is concerned, so that in our present discussion we are obliged to start from one of the two hypotheses that are put forward regarding it, the Mechanistic and the Organic; and since the one or the other of these hypotheses is, in our present state of knowledge, a necessary starting point for any complete world-view of evolution, I shall suspend for a few pages the development of the specific time-picture which we have begun, in order to give a brief statement of the two hypotheses.

I am aware of the danger in attempting an abridged statement of these two opposing views. One finds so many variations in the various presentations of the two theories by writers who are in professed agreement that it would be vanity to think of being able to make any abstract of either theory that would win the unanimous assent of its supporters. Each writer of any consequence makes some modification of his predecessors' views, and adds something of his own, and the reader's own view is altered somewhat by each new book, so that he is often not sure of how to state his own position. If asked, e.g., whether I am a "creative" or "emergent" evolutionist, I would answer "both," though that might appear to some as a hopelessly non-discriminative answer. All I can do here is to give a succinct statement of my own understanding of the two different views and incur the ensuing risks.

CHAPTER II

THE MECHANISTIC HYPOTHESIS

I have spoken of variations sometimes as if they were
due to chance. This is a wholly incorrect expression;
it merely serves to acknowledge plainly our ignorance
of the cause of each particular variation.—DARWIN.

❖　　❖　　❖　　❖

BOTH THE MECHANISTIC AND THE ORGANIC HYPOTH-
eses agree that in the world as it stands at present we
find not only matter, but also life, mind, and purpose.
The mechanistic hypothesis, however, as I understand it, holds that this earth was originally a purely
inorganic world without life, mind, or purpose, gov-
erned by purely mechanical laws alone; and that at
some point of time in the relatively recent past, life
got started upon the surface of this mechanical world
by some kind of "biological accident," and having got
started in "one or more primordial forms" it then set
out on a course of evolution impelled by a strong
reproductive impulse, presumably co-accidental with
life itself; and with a strong tendency to reproduce
or repeat the type, coupled with a lesser tendency to
slight variations and an occasional tendency to a great
variation, it gradually differentiated its "one or more
primordial forms" into many genera and species of
life, each species or genus then moving forward

towards greater and greater perfection under the operation of "natural selection," until we have the multi-variegated organic world as we find it to-day.

Upon this hypothesis the non-vital material world is alone basic and permanent. Life, mind, and purpose are temporary phases which have come into existence in some accidental or unknown way at a certain point of time, and which may disappear again at some future time through the mindless and purposeless operation of the mechanical laws of the basic non-vital material world. In the meantime, to preserve a consistent world-unity, life, mind, and purpose must be explained, so far, at least, as scientific explanation is possible, by mechanistic laws similar to those which operate in the purely physical world.

This might be loosely called the neo-Darwinian hypothesis; though Darwin himself remained inclined either towards a dualistic view—the original creation of some "simple archetypal creature," with the possibility of subsequent differentiations under chance variation and natural selection—as indicated, for example, in the closing paragraph of the *Origin of Species,* or towards a suspended judgment about it, as in the sentences quoted at the beginning of this chapter.

There are, however, some difficulties in the hypothesis that should be noted here. In the first place, nearly all the significant words used to set out the theory were originally merely tentative terms used of necessity to *describe* processes that were as yet inexplicable. But these tentative terms by repetition and consequent familiarity have tended more and more to become accepted as *explanations* of the phenomena rather than tentative descriptions. Hence their tendency to obscure or conceal without explaining the problem.

The word "accident," for example, when used with reference to the first appearance of life, may imply either that (1) the first phenomenon of life had actually no causal connection with the pre-life matter of the world, or only that (2) the causal connections are not yet discovered. If the former is implied, then it stands in contradiction to the fundamental assumption of all science, namely, that every event has a cause. If the second, then it is merely an admission of present ignorance. In neither case does it give any explanation of the phenomenon; but by frequent repetition of the word we get into the habit of thinking that it is an explanation.

Again "reproductive impulse" merely *names* an essential factor in life without explaining it. An explanation would involve some knowledge of the origin and significance of this "impulse." When, how, why did this impulse get into the world-machinery? The tendency, however, is to accept the name as if it were an explanation. Similarly a "tendency to variation" comes to be accepted as an explanation, so that the mind stops short of the real and scientific questions:

Where did the "tendency" come from, and what is its role in world history; what causes the "variation," and for what purpose? Are these also to be described as "accidental," and, if so, what does the term specifically mean? Did the "tendency" and "variation" originally come without a cause, or did they emerge from some causal source as yet undiscovered? And where are the "tendency" and the "variation" leading to?

It becomes obvious, when examined closely, that this first hypothesis of an original world of purely non-vital matter, if tested by the standards of other knowledge, is not even a tentative explanation of the origin of life. Darwin himself was fully aware of this, as is shown in the closing sentences of the *Origin of Species,* where, in a very memorable last paragraph, he sums up the view of the world which he has developed in detail through four hundred-odd pages.

It is interesting to contemplate a tangled bank, clothed with many plants of many kinds, with birds singing on the bushes, with various insects flitting about, and with worms crawling through the damp earth, and to reflect that these elaborately constructed forms, so different from each other, and dependent upon each other in so complex a manner, have all been produced by laws acting around us. These laws, taken in the largest sense, being Growth with Reproduction; Inheritance, which is almost implied by reproduction; Variability from the indirect and direct action of the conditions of life, and from use and disuse; a Ratio of Increase so high as to lead to a Struggle for Life, and as a consequence to Natural Selection, entailing Divergence of Character and Extinction of less improved forms. Thus, from the war of nature, from famine and death, the most exalted object which we are capable of conceiving, namely, the production of the higher animals, directly follows. There is grandeur in this view of life, with its several powers, having been originally breathed by the Creator into a few forms or into one; and that, while this planet has gone cycling on according to the fixed law of gravity, from so simple a beginning endless forms most beautiful and most wonderful have been and are being evolved.

The significant words in this paragraph, from our point of view, are: "this view of life, with its several powers, *having been originally breathed by the Creator into a few forms or into one.*" Darwin apparently saw that this, *or something akin to it,* was an essential link in the spiral chain of his evolution theory, the link between lifeless and living forms. Some Neo-Darwinians, I fancy, might explain this phrase of Darwin's as either a conciliatory concession to contemporary opinion, or as a carry-over from his pre-scientific religious beliefs, which he was not yet quite ready (1859) to abandon, but which the more confident of the mechanistic scientists of the present time would naturally reject as an inconsistent ingredient.

To one, however, who tries to work out a concrete philosophical view of the world as a whole, on the basis of a time-evolution of all its forms from matter to man, the mechanistic hypothesis appears at the present juncture to obscure the real problem of the beginnings of life by taking on the semblance of an explanation without the reality. The large and increasing acceptance of this hypothesis during the present century, at least on the American continent, is due, I think, first, to its reiterated claims of being the only thoroughgoing scientific method of explanation, and second, to the general revolt against the old dogma of external design and direction, a revolt which has rather outlived its usefulness.

CHAPTER III

THE ORGANIC HYPOTHESIS

It is a long way from granite to the oyster; farther yet to Plato and the preaching of the immortality of the soul. Yet all must come as surely as the first atom has two sides.—EMERSON, *Nature,* 1841.

How can purposive forms of organization arise without a purposive working cause? How can work full of design build itself up without a design and without a builder?—KANT, *The General History of Nature,* 1755.

But there can be no reasonable doubt that living matter, in due process of time, originated from non-living; and if that be so, we must push our conclusion farther, and believe that not only living matter, but all matter, is associated with something of the same general description as mind in the higher animals. We come, that is, to a monistic conclusion, in that we believe that there is only one fundamental substance, and that this possesses not only material properties, but also properties for which the word *mental* is the nearest approach.—JULIAN HUXLEY, *Essays of a Biologist,* 1926.

❖   ❖   ❖   ❖

1. *The Attest of Logic*

THE ORGANIC HYPOTHESIS HOLDS THAT THE WORLD was at no time of its evolution a merely purposeless

131

mechanical world, in which matter was prior to mind in the time order. The real original world was already and always a world of matter, life, mind, and purpose, actual or latent. Matter on this hypothesis is regarded not as an independent substance in its own right, but as the means or material through which the life and mind of the world works itself out from its potential to its actual destiny. The life-force, or mind-force, or whatever we may call it in its earlier stages, works within the sensuous material of the world, and gradually shapes and moulds this material first into what we now call inorganic formations, and then, in the ripeness of time and environment, into those organic forms in which the life-principle rises into recognizable living shapes, and emerges into actual objective existence. On this view evolution through the reproductive impulse, the persistence of the general type with certain tendencies to variation, natural selection, etc., is not the directing agency, but the *method* by which the directing agency, the life-and-mind force, works itself out to actuality.

Upon this hypothesis life, mind, and purpose are not temporary and accidental, but basic and permanent elements in the world; potential and latent— so far at least as human perception upon this planet is concerned—in the first æons of their history, and emerging to actuality at a certain point of time in the world evolution. With the actual emergence of these new phases of the world there emerge also new

principles of activity that were not in objective operation in the pre-life period of the world, and whose
mode of working could not have been predicted by
any human study of non-living matter.

This view does not stand in contradiction to the
mechanistic laws of nature. The mechanistic laws are
considered as the means by which the vital force advances from potential to actual life-forms. I call it
"vital force" because one has to use some known term
to describe it, and while its inner nature is still unknown, this term seems to come closer to a description of its objective behaviour than any other term
we have. That the vital force, the life principle, works
by mechanical means which biology, physiology, etc.,
are busy exploring, is no evidence at all that the vital
force itself is mechanistic, in the accepted connotation of that word; and to call a living organ a "mechanism," in the same sense as one would speak about
a machine, seems a sheer confusion or denial of significant characteristics by which we distinguish one
thing from another.

This modern error—for so, at least, it seems to
me—of characterizing life-activity as mechanism
seems to have arisen from a too exclusive concentra-
tion (*a*) upon the causal relations among the various
physical parts within the individual organism itself,
and (*b*) upon the relation between the individual
organism and its physical environment, until by the
mere accumulation of the details of these physical

causal relations, internal and external, the central unifying life-force is buried out of sight. Eventually the life-force itself, too elusive to be caught by the mechanical mode of investigation, and now hidden from view under the growing mass of details of its external behaviour, is denied altogether, and the aggregate of its behaviouristic relations substituted for it. This is an easy but unsatisfactory method of disposing of the most difficult element in the whole problem.

When, for example, a dog crosses a street, you have forty pounds of matter moved and directed by an automatic force within the dog's skin. When the dog is suddenly killed by an automobile you have the same size, shape, and avoirdupois of matter lying upon the street, still subject to all the mechanistic laws of non-vital matter, but without any powers now of moving itself from within. It can be moved now only by contact with physical force from without. The inner life-force that formerly moved it from within, without any impact from material force from without, is gone. The difference is enormous; as great as any difference which comes within the realm of knowledge. To call this life-force mechanistic in the same sense as the disintegrating chemical changes that are now going on within the dog's dead body are mechanistic, or in the sense in which the dog's dead body may be moved by an external force, is merely, as we have said, to confuse all those boundaries of knowledge by which we differentiate one phase of reality from another. Life or life-force may have to be redefined so as to show more closely its connection with the mechanistic forces of the matter through which it works, but to discard the word because the common connotation is now not sufficiently precise, and to replace it by a word that refers primarily to lifeless relations, can afford no help to clear thinking, unless its temporary use and its felt inadequacy may operate as the gadfly for stimulating the mind to a new definition of the old term "life."

This second hypothesis, that life, mind, and purpose are permanent elements in the world, though their emergence in individualized objective forms may have occurred at a particular point of time in world evolution, on this planet at least, is the hypothesis which I have adopted here, because it appears the more scientific and logical, and is more in accord with our complete experience of the world at the present time. Upon this view the emergence of living forms upon the earth's surface would be neither a miracle nor an accident, but a next causal advance, predestined by some creative and purposive energy inherent in the world, in the evolution of life and mind from its potential to its actual existence. While this is a hypothesis only and not an explanation of the emergence of life and mind any more than is the mechanistic view, it does leave the way open for a logical explanation without any break in the cause-

and-effect sequence. It is the hypothesis put forward by Kant, the first of the moderns, as already observed, to give vital expression to the evolutionary theory as an explanation of the present world of living forms.

Though Kant was a mechanist within the realm of knowledge which encompassed, as he put it, the "phenomenal" world (*The Critique of Pure Reason,* 1781), he saw that mechanistic categories could not explain all experience, and especially the obligations of duty; and so he postulated a "noumenal" world (*The Critique of Practical Reason,* 1788), which lay beyond the boundaries of cause-and-effect knowledge, but was nevertheless real, and related to the "phenomenal" world through a unifying purposiveness. His summarized statement of the hypothesis regarding the generation of the organic world under a purposive force is worth quoting here because it is one of the earliest statements we have of the theory, and because it appears in Kant's last book, *The Critique of Judgment* (1790), the "coping-stone," as he said, of his philosophy, and is his final judgment after a long life of devotion to science and philosophy.

Here [he says], it is permissible for the Archaeologist of nature to derive from the surviving traces of its oldest revolutions, according to all its mechanism known or supposed by him, the great family of creatures (for so we must represent them if the said thoroughgoing relationship is to have any ground) which exists in the world to-day. He can suppose the bosom of mother earth, as she passed out of her chaotic state (like a great animal) to have given birth in the beginning to creatures of less purposive form, that these again gave birth to others which formed themselves with greater adaptation to their place of birth and their relations to each other; until this womb, becoming torpid and ossified, limited its births to definite species not further modifiable, and the manifoldness remained as it was at the end of the operation of that formative period—only he must still in the end ascribe to this universal mother an organization purposive in respect of all these creatures; otherwise it would not be possible to think the possibility of the purposive form of the products of the animal and vegetable kingdom. He has then only pushed further back the ground of explanation and cannot pretend to have made the development of those two kingdoms independent of the condition of final causes.[1]

Kant's view here, if one can simplify it by explanatory paraphrase, is that all the specific forms which we find in the world to-day were produced by the purposive activity of a mind-force working in and through the sensuous matter of the world, and shaping out these diversified organic forms as the means of realizing in an objective way its own potential destiny. In other words, Kant believed that the present manifold differentiated forms of the world are the result of a complete and thoroughgoing inner purposiveness of the world, working its way, especially in

[1] This paragraph follows upon the paragraph quoted from Kant above, p. 72.

its early history, upward and outward through sensuous matter, from the lowest forms of organic life
up to and into the life of man. In man, however, this
inner inconscious purposiveness emerges to consciousness and begins to work now, through man's brain
and hand, in an explicitly purposive manner upon
the matter of the world, imposing new purposive
forms upon this matter now from the outside (the
artificial world, or world of art, as we now call it),
as contrasted with the purposive forms (the organic
forms of nature) previously shaped by the same purposive activity of the world working embryonically,
as we might say, from the inside.

Upon this view the plant, the tree, the bird, the
animal, and man, are the forms which the world by
its creative activity has shaped into these objective
expressions of its own evolving life. Professor Haldane
has in a different form expressed the same view, as I
understand him, in *Mechanism, Life, and Personality,*
where he maintains that when the present investigations of the problem are eventually carried out to
their completion it will most likely be found that
instead of mechanical law giving the explanation to
life and mind, it will be life and mind and personality
which will eventually give the explanation and significance of mechanical law and of what is now called
inorganic matter. According to this view, then, with
the actual emergence of life in individual organic
forms upon the earth's surface, the world advanced

to a new phase of its evolution. Life, mind, and purpose, latent and potential in the preorganic period, emerge to actuality in the organic world, in an ascending series from plant to man.

Professor A. N. Whitehead, who, like Kant, is both a scientist and a philosopher, expresses in a paragraph the same view as Kant regarding the purposive nature of the world, and it is interesting to see the two paragraphs side by side with an interval of some hundred and forty years between.

There is clear evidence that certain operations of certain animal bodies depend upon the foresight of an end and the purpose to attain it. It is no solution of the problem to ignore this evidence because other operations have been explained in terms of physical and chemical laws. The existence of a problem is not even acknowledged. It is vehemently denied. Many a scientist has patiently designed experiments for the *purpose* of substantiating his belief that animal operations are motivated by no purposes. He has perhaps spent his spare time in writing articles to prove that human beings are as other animals so that "purpose" is a category irrelevant for the explanation of their bodily activities, his own included. Scientists animated by the purpose of proving that they are purposeless constitute an interesting subject for study.

2. *The Intuition of Poetry*

Shall we not maintain, then, that Mind is the first origin and moving power of all that is, or has been, or will be, since it has been clearly shown that Mind is the source of change and motion in all things?—PLATO, *The Laws, c.* 360 B.C.

> Even then I felt
> Gleams like the flashing of a shield; the earth
> And common face of Nature spake to me
> Rememberable things.
> WORDSWORTH, *The Prelude,* Book I, 1798.

This conception of a vital purposive principle in the world received its first powerful intuitive expression in English literature in Wordsworth's *Prelude,* a poem whose significance and originality in relation to modern views of the world are not yet fully realized. In this poem Wordsworth labours by all the devices of language—by concrete illustration, by philosophic exposition, by poetry—to convey his knowledge (for so he calls it) of the organic and spiritual unity of the world which has been revealed to him through often repeated mystic experiences; a knowledge, however, which, in the end, he confesses to be incommunicable through the ordinary resources of words, except to the kindred mystic whose own personal experience can piece together the broken arches of common speech. It is the knowledge of immediate contact. "I have *felt* a presence" is the statement which he reiterates with many variations throughout the *Prelude.* His thought, expressed in cold prose, is that Man is the apex of the pyramidal world structure, where the Mind which permeates the whole fabric emerges to the light of consciousness, and, in

the organism and mind of man, becomes the inheritor
of all its own lower manifestations from the base to
the top of the pyramid. But to Wordsworth the Mind
which comes out so clearly at the apex is already
present and stirring at the very base, and may be *felt*
there by the sensitive mind of man, though hidden
from the reach of sense. This view of a living world,
even in that portion of it which to sense appears as
non-living matter, Wordsworth deduced from his own
living contact with it, repeated in countless experiences from childhood, youth, and manhood. He gave
the first powerful expression of the view when he was
twenty-eight years old, in the now familiar though
often unapprehended lines:

> And I have felt
> A presence that disturbs me with the joy
> Of elevated thoughts; a sense sublime
> Of something far more deeply interfused,
> Whose dwelling is the light of setting suns,
> And the round ocean and the living air,
> And the blue sky, and in the mind of man;
> A motion and a spirit, that impels
> All thinking things, all objects of all thought,
> And rolls through all things.

It should be noticed that the "presence" which he
feels is a living "something" which exists not only in
the "mind of man," but in the "round ocean" and the
"blue sky," and is discoverable through its immediate
cause-and-effect relation with his own mind. The "joy

of elevated thoughts," which he has experienced not
once but hundreds of times, is an effect, indubitable
and profoundly significant, of which the "blue sky"
is the cause; and where others stop with the fact
Wordsworth presses on for the scientific interpretation of the fact. The "joy of elevated thoughts" is a
mental effect, and he deduces that the "blue sky" and
the "round ocean," which are its cause, and which to
the senses and sense instruments appear as mindless
phenomena, are in reality animated by mind, whose
influences, while dead to the physical senses, are ap-
propriable to the sensitive mind of man through immediate feeling. "I have *felt* a *presence*," he says. All
of us have felt in varying degrees the same influences
from what we call, from the sense level, inanimate
nature, the sudden reinvigorating influence, for example, of a sunset after a fatiguing day's work in-
doors. But while, as I have said, most of us are con-
tented with the fact, Wordsworth probed for the
interpretation, and the unique value and originality
of his great nature poetry, 1798–1808, is due, first, to
his vivid experiences of the mental joys offered us by
nature; second, to his scientific questionings about
their cause; and third, to his confidence that other
less sensitive minds may, under the guidance of his
poetry, become richer sharers of these joys by consciously seeking them. To indoor people whose minds
are perturbed by "the many shapes of joyless daylight
. . . the fretful stir unprofitable and the fever of the

world," in a word, by all the vanities that seem inseparable from human society, Wordsworth reiterates in poem after poem the invitation:

> Come forth, and bring with you a heart
> That watches and receives.

At a later period, 1814, when his vivid experiences of the mental nature of the entire world had decayed to little more than a memory of things that were, he gave a more explicitly philosophic, though less poetic, statement of his views:

> To every Form of being is assigned
> An *active*[1] Principle:—howe'er removed
> From sense and observation, it subsists
> In all things, in all natures; in the stars
> Of azure heaven, the unenduring clouds,
> In flower and tree, in every pebbly stone
> That paves the brooks, the stationary rocks,
> The moving waters, and the invisible air.
> Whate'er exists hath properties that spread
> Beyond itself, communicating good,
> A simple blessing, or with evil mixed;
> Spirit that knows no insulated spot,
> No chasm, no solitude; from link to link
> It circulates, the Soul of all the worlds.
> This is the freedom of the universe;
> Unfolded still the more, more visible,
> The more we know; and yet is reverenced least,
> And least respected in the human Mind,
> Its most apparent home.
> > *The Excursion,* Book ix.

[1] The italics are Wordsworth's.

While this "active Principle" is not so "apparent" in the lower orders of nature as it is in the human mind, yet it may be *felt* everywhere throughout the realm of nature, if its awakened human form, man, is sensitive to mental affinities.

Wordsworth also had an unalterable conviction that this "active Principle" was a permanent and indestructible element in the world structure, as is shown in the following rather remarkable lines:

> Should the whole frame of earth by inward throes
> Be wrenched, or fire come down from far to scorch
> Her pleasant habitations, and dry up
> Old Ocean, in his bed left singed and bare,
> Yet would the living Presence still subsist
> Victorious, and composure would ensue,
> And kindlings like the morning—presage sure
> Of day returning and of life revived.
>   *The Prelude,* Book v.

These lines express an integral element of the organic hypothesis which we have been discussing in this chapter.

The main characteristic of Wordsworth's interpretation of the world in *The Prelude* is that he carries the scientific method farther forward than do the scientists, beyond the bounds of matter into the realm of mind. He experiences, for example, a memorable stimulus of joy from the sight of the "floating cloud." This experience, as noted in a parallel passage above, is an effect of which the floating cloud is the cause. But the experience is fundamentally a mental one, and he reasons that the cause is also a mental reality, though embodied in a physical phenomenon, the cloud, and transmitted to the mind through the physical eye and the physical filaments that connect the eye with the cloud. Mind, to him, on the ground of cause and effect, is a *real* presence, not only in man, but also in nature, though its activity in nature—at least below the animal sphere—is not palpable to sense perception. *The Prelude,* as Coleridge pointed out, is fundamentally a philosophical poem, and is in a very real sense the original English text upon which all the expository work on creative or emergent evolution of the present century has been based, however unconscious the expositors may have been of Wordsworth's pioneer work in the field.

The laboratory scientist may be inclined to discount the poet's evidence here on the ground that it is based on mystic or intuitive insight rather than on scientific observation and analysis. But Wordsworth was a close scientific observer and reasoner as well as a mystic, and in all original work both faculties are necessary. What makes Plato the greatest of all philosophers is the fine commingling of steady observation and logical reasoning with a penetrative mystic insight. In the *Ion,* for example, Plato, by his mystic insight, brings us to the very life and springs of poetry which Aristotle misses entirely by his purely analytic method in the *Poetics*. As Bertrand Russell says in his illuminating essay on *Mysticism and Logic:*

> The greatest men who have been philosophers have felt the need of both science and mysticism. . . . Reason is a harmonizing controlling force rather than a creative one. Even in the most purely logical realm, it is insight that first arrives at what is new.

In returning in the next chapter to the reconstruction of the time-picture of the evolution of the living forms in the world which we suspended two chapters back, I shall assume the organic hypothesis outlined above as the background for the construction of the picture. The concrete picture itself, however, is in no way hypothetical, but is drawn from empirical observation and objective evidence, and is submitted for scientific examination quite independent of the metaphysical hypothesis submitted above as a probable ultimate basis and explanation of the picture.

CHAPTER IV

THE EMERGENCE OF ORGANIC LIFE: THE TIME-PICTURE CONTINUED

All changes pass without violence, by reason of the two cardinal conditions of boundless space and boundless time. Geology has initiated us into the secularity of nature, and has taught us to disuse our dame-school measures, and exchange our Mosaic and Ptolemaic schemes for her large style. . . . Now we learn what patient periods must round themselves before the rock is formed, then before the rock is broken and the first lichen race has disintegrated the thinnest external plate into soil, and opened the door for the remote Flora, Fauna, Ceres, and Pomona to come in. How far off yet is the trilobite! how far the quadruped! how inconceivably remote is Man! Yet all duly arrive.—EMERSON, *Nature,* 1841.

◇　　◇　　◇　　◇

THE ENTIRE PHENOMENON OF THE ORGANIC WORLD divides itself by its external behaviour into three well-defined classes, plant life, animal life, and man, each class with new and original characteristics of its own. To trace and mark these new characteristics as they emerge in their time-evolution upwards through plant and animal life to where the life-and-mind of the world eventually emerges from its unfreed and inconscious activity to its freed and conscious activity in the life and mind of man, is our next step.

I shall not attempt any analytic definition of either life or mind, though that would be germane to our present purpose if it could be done; nor any discussion of the detailed material structure or processes of life from the biological or physiological point of view, as that would fall outside our present purpose. While biologists have learned much of the material organism through which life manifests itself, they have not yet hit upon the thing itself, the life-principle, or whatever we may call it, that animates and unifies the organism. Some of them, as we have seen, hold it to be merely a mechanistic principle, others a vital formative principle, so that as far as *knowledge* is concerned the question is still in the realm of conjecture. I only wish to trace and describe some of the significant ways in which the life-principle manifests itself in its objective appearance and behaviour as we follow its evolution through an ascending series from lower to higher life-forms, and eventually to the highest form we know—man.

By tracing the Time-picture in this way, and noting the new significant characteristics as they emerge in the ascending scale, we shall be able to see more distinctly the actual emergence and peculiar nature of the mental power in man that gave birth to language. The treatment will consist, as indicated above, in a series of descriptions of the significant forms and behaviour of the three cardinal classes of life: plant, animal, and man.

1. *Plant Life*

When life emerges in the vegetable world it emerges as an active and formative energy, with the power of gathering and forming a given quantity of matter into a certain predetermined and self-determining shape. J. S. Haldane writes of it thus: "Life manifests itself in two ways—as *structure* and as *activity*. But we also recognize—a biologist feels it in his very bones—that this is *living* structure and *living* activity." In order to work more directly to the end in view here, I shall substitute for Haldane's "structure" and "activity" the two words "individuality" and "freedom," and change his sentence to read: "Life manifests itself in two ways—as *individuality* and as *freedom*," and add that as we ascend the life series those two features become more pronounced and significant. "Individuality" includes "structure," but connotes also, a little more explicitly, unity and definite boundaries. "Freedom," as used above, is almost synonymous with "living activity," except that it connotes a little more pointedly the idea of liberation, *in a certain sense,* from mechanical law. But a more explicit and positive definition of the two terms may help towards clearness.

By "individuality" I mean that the delimited piece

of matter which we call the plant has within itself an active and formative life-principle which draws around itself a certain quantity of stuff from its natural environment, and organizes this into its own body with a definite and limited material form, whose parts have not only a definite spatial relation to each other, but are actively and vitally maintained in that relation. A quantity of inorganic matter, a stone, for example, has no individuality in the sense of *actively* related parts, whose spatial relations to each other depend upon the continuance of a vital unifying principle within the particular body. Break the stone into two parts, and the shape of each half and the spatial relations of the parts within each half remain the same. Cut a branch from an individual tree, on the other hand, so as to sever it from the unifying and form-sustaining life-principle, and thus abandon it to the influences of mechanical laws alone, and in a given time these mechanical forces will destroy the definite formation of its parts and reduce its substance to formless matter. In the tree an active principle has emerged to visible actuality, that does not appear as actual in what we call non-living matter, though the formative energy which produced the tree must, as it seems to me, have been latent in the pre-life matter, according to all our conceptions of cause

By attributing "freedom" to the plant I mean that a new principle of activity has come to life within the and effect.

material organism with a power of motion and work from its own centre, thus rising in some sense above the operation of mere mechanical law and mechanical motions, as we know these at present, where objects are moved only by external impact. The motions of an inorganic object, a stone, are determined solely by mechanical laws such as gravitation. Left unsupported in the air it will drop to the ground; placed in water it will sink; set on an inclined plane it will roll to the bottom. In all cases its motion can be predicted by mechanical calculations.

An organic object, on the other hand, a tree for example, manifests a new principle of motion as it organizes and raises its form and matter out of and above the earth's surface. This motion is originated and carried on from within the tree, not from without, and this new kind of motion could not have been predicted by any study of non-living matter previous to the appearance of plant life. In this self-active upward movement there is a certain liberation of this individualized living piece of matter from bare mechanical law, for the tree in a given time will organize several tons of matter into its own tree-substance and raise this up several feet above the earth's surface in opposition, for example, to the law of gravity. No non-living object has the power of raising itself in this way.

As our language stands at present this new power of self-motion from within is best described as a mode of *freedom* to distinguish it from motion by impact from without, which we designate as mechanical motion. Something like this we are obliged to do if we are to describe characteristic differences at all.

But this new motion of freedom is not a cancellation of the lower mechanical laws. The tree in its free movement upward is dependent, for example, upon the law of gravity for the very rise which it makes above the law. It raises its trunk perpendicularly in obedience to the law and depends upon the constancy of the law for the steadiness of its rise. It uses also many other mechanical laws—which botanical science investigates—as the means by which it accomplishes its growth, maintains its life, and realizes in this way its own particular degree of freedom; and it depends upon the constancy of all these mechanical laws in order to rise to freedom at all. The freedom of organized plant life is thus not so much a freedom *from* mechanical law as it is a freedom obtained *by means of* mechanical law.

2. *Animal Life*

In the emergence to animal life the world advances to a new cycle in its evolution, embodies its life-energies in a more highly organized and self-contained individuality with a higher degree of freedom. In this new cycle three new characteristics emerge to actuality that have significance in our Time-picture:

mind, self-motion, and *purposive sound,* or inarticulate language, as we usually call it for want of an exact name of its own. We shall consider these three in the order set down.

(a) Mind

What is mind? For the approach to language this question can be better answered by comparative description than by analytic definition; and I shall attempt now to describe *mind* in its objective appearance and behaviour in relation to space-and-time, by comparison and contrast with *body* as represented in the lower cycle of plant life, where mind does not yet explicitly appear.

The tree, as noted above, has an organized and self-contained individuality with an active power of selecting sensuous material from its environment, synthesizing this into its own individual form, and actively maintaining it in that synthesis. But its individuality does not extend, as we might say, beyond its own bark. It is contained within its own physical dimensions and stands confined to its own particular physical point in space and time. There is no perceptible power within the tree of reaching beyond its own physical boundaries, so that it does not differ significantly in that respect from any inorganic material object. It has, in other words, no actualized mind.

In the animal, on the other hand, the new and unique power of mind has actually emerged from the creative and, as I think, purposive energies of the world. The animal has the same power of active assimilation and growth as the tree. Its body has similar limited and defined physical dimensions. But centred within its body is the new power which we now call *mind,* which, through the avenues of the sense-organs of sight, hearing, and smelling, radiates or reaches out a certain distance into space and time, beyond the body's limits, so that the animal's individuality, by this new power of mind, extends beyond its own skin, beyond its own material body, and holds in its mental grasp, and actually occupies mentally, a much larger space-and-time environment than the body occupies. In contrast with the plant whose individuality is confined to its own physical dimensions and which is thence confined to a physical world alone, the animal with its double body-and-mind nature lives in a double physical-and-mental world. The new phenomenon of mind and its correspondent mental world emerge together.

This mental world which emerges as the habitation of this new power of mind in animal life is a nonmaterial world which transcends the laws of the material world and the material bodies in it, as for example the law that two bodies cannot simultaneously occupy the same point of space. The living physical body in which the mind centres is subject to

all the laws of the physical world as is any non-living
material body; but the mind radiates, as we said, into
a much larger region, so that the minds of two animals whose bodies occupy mutually exclusive regions
of space can occupy a common mutually inclusive
mental region. The difference between the two can
be made objectively clear by an illustration, as also
the difference between the plant and the animal with
respect to this new power of mind.

The two trees A and B stand separated from one
another in mutually exclusive regions of space, the

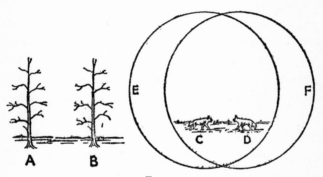

Fig. 1

individuality of each confined within itself. The physical bodies of the two animals, C and D, are in a similar way mutually exclusive. But the individualized
mind, though centred or focused in the space-and-
time-bound body, extends into the larger region represented by the circumferences of the two circles,
E and F, and these two mental worlds are not mu-

tually exclusive. The greater portion of the occupied circles is common mental ground. This is a new phenomenon in the world that could not have been predicted by any study of non-mental organic objects.

Whether we are to speak of the animal's mind as *confined within* its own body and *looking out* upon this larger world; or as merely centred or focused within the body and *actually extending* to the larger circumference, may be largely a matter of agreement upon the connotation of words. The latter, however, is the more accurate description of the phenomenon of mind. It is also in more direct agreement with Kant's exposition of space and time, as I understand Kant. But however we may describe it, it is clear that in animal existence the creative life-force of the world has produced individualized material organisms through which, as physical space-time centres, the mind of the world emerges into some kind of individual consciousness of its surrounding environment of space and time, and takes some kind of mental possession of this.

(b) Self-Motion

Corresponding with its unique environing world of mind the animal has the new and unique power of self-motion. By means of this creative power of motion within its own body, initiated, controlled, and directed by the mind, the animal can move itself from place to place within its larger mental world, and take successive physical possession of it.

But in this new movement of the world towards freedom in animal life there is no cancellation of lower laws. The squirrel by its own power of motion from within, coupled with the law of gravity that keeps its feet firm upon the ground, can go up an inclined plane while the stone on the same plane will roll to the bottom. But the same law which takes the stone down enables the squirrel to go up. The animal's freedom rests upon the constancy of mechanical law. Similarly, the squirrel could not continue to subsist were it not that the oak tree remained constant to its own oak-tree laws in producing acorns for the squirrel to eat.

To speak in this way of the oak producing acorns for the squirrel to eat may at first sight seem like attributing an unwarranted purposiveness to the system of nature. It is, admittedly, an external and bald way of putting it, and yet one can see no other alternative if one attempts to think out in detailed completeness the idea of the organic unity of the world. We are accustomed to think of the oak tree producing acorns to fulfil its own nature in reproducing and maintaining itself, rather than to feed the squirrels; and to say that the squirrel must adjust himself to this nature of the tree, and to his environment in general, if he wishes to subsist. That *seems* the solider way of putting it because the environment seems a much more durable, solid, and intractable thing than does any small animal species like the squirrel that subsists within it. But this appearance is surely due to the deception of the senses, and to a dualistic mode of thinking. As soon as the observer begins to think and speak particularly of a single small animal like the squirrel this animal immediately stands out alone in his mind in its smallness and apparent insignificance against the entire and durable background of nature, and the observer, with these two unequal opposites objectively in his eye, forgets for the moment the organic unity of the world which he theoretically asserts as the whole basis of his thinking, and thinks and speaks of the squirrel adjusting itself in an external way to its environment. He forgets for the time that the environment and the squirrel are only differentiated elements in a single self-differentiating world, whose life and mind are gradually emerging into concrete actuality through an ascending series of differentiated organic forms, where the higher cycle is, in each step, conditioned by and dependent upon the lower; and that the world unfolding itself in this way could not have produced and sustained the more highly individualized life-organism of the squirrel with its power of self-motion, its senses, its finer assimilative organs, its half-freed, half-conscious mind, until it had first developed the plant life with its power of modifying the nutritive substance of the inorganic world over into that intermediated state, acorns, etc., that could be assimilated as food by the more finely wrought organisms of animal life. The world, though unfolding itself as a hierarchy in the successive steps of its evolution, appears, nevertheless, as a single, not a multiple, world, each higher order resting upon, supported by, and evolving from the one beneath. Conceiving it this way, it seems more consistent to think of the creative world-force as evolving and directing the lower order, plant life, for example, with a view to the subsequent evolution and sustenance of the higher order of animal life, than to think of the animal as adjusting itself to the lower plant order, when that lower order must have been already adjusted both to the prospective life and subsequent sustenance of the animal before the animal could have come into existence at all or have any prospect of continuing to exist. The squirrel does not in fact adjust himself to his environment except in the most meagre degree. On the contrary he finds the environment already adjusted to his needs, and requires only a rudimentary instruction as to how to appropriate what he requires from this preadjusted environment.

(c) Purposive Sound

The third unique characteristic which, in the evolution of the life-force of the world, emerges to actuality now for the first time in animal life is *purposive sound,* the cry or call by which one animal communicates with another. Mechanical sound which is made by external impact among solid or semi-solid material bodies expresses no purpose. It is the effect of the physical impact, and merely reports what has happened or is happening. Hence it has significance only in reference to the past or concurrent present. The call of an animal is also no doubt a report of the animal's present or immediate past state, but its chief significance is its reference to the future, towards some effect of which it is the intentional or purposive cause. The call of the wolf, for example, to rally the hunting pack. It explicitly anticipates time. In this way as expressing explicit purpose it resembles the language of man, and Darwin, as observed above, has actually established the habit of calling it language. But being inarticulate it is not really language, as I hope to show more clearly a little farther on, so I shall use a new word and call this purposive sound of animal-life "rudi-language," to distinguish it from mechanical and non-purposive sound on the one hand and from language on the other.

This rudi-language of the animals is the natural accompaniment of mind and locomotion. The three appear as being teleologically related. With the individualized mind which holds an expanse of space beyond the body's limits, and with the power of self-movement to take, in a given time, successive physical possession of this larger expanse, the animals have vocal organs by which they can produce these significant sounds for purpose of intercommunication within the larger expanse of their mental world, and for mutual physical co-operation within it. The plant, having no mind nor locomotion, has no language. The three things emerge together.

CHAPTER V

ANIMAL INTELLIGENCE AND EXPRESSION

> The goal of truth lies in a single point from which
> we can survey all sides and discover that no animal
> can invent language, that no God must invent it, and
> that man as a human being can and must invent it.—
> HERDER, *Origin of Language,* 1772.

❖   ❖   ❖   ❖

1. *Animal Cries and Language*

SINCE THESE ANIMAL CRIES OR SOUNDS HAVE PURPOSIVE SIGNIFI-
cances similar to that of language, in what respect do
they differ from language? I shall try to give a definite answer to this question.

First, they are inarticulate while language is articulate. And what precisely does "inarticulate" mean?
It means (1) that these cries are not explicitly articulated sounds with clear-edged beginnings, middles,
and endings, as are the word-sounds "h-a-p" and
"h-o-p," or "d-i-g" and "d-i-p," so that one sound can
be clearly and definitely differentiated from another;
and (2), as a corollary to this, the sounds have no
conventional meanings; that is, they are not invested
each with an arbitrary and definite connotation quite
apart from any natural sound-suggestion which they

may have, so that one sound stands exclusively for one thing, another sound for another thing, as do the words of language like "wolf" and "bear." In other words, the animals' cries are natural cries as distinguished from the conventionalized sounds which we call words, and they have the characteristic vagueness or indefiniteness of significance which all natural sounds have. In this respect of natural vagueness of significance the cries of animals resemble the mechanical sounds in nature, though differing from these in expressing purpose. They resemble also in this respect the vagueness of instrumental music which is expressed also in natural mechanical sounds which have no explicit definiteness for the mind.

Some more specific characteristics of the animal cries should be set down here to remove any possible ambiguity.

(1) It is true that the animal or bird does, as Darwin and other naturalists have pointed out, utter several natural cries that can be distinguished from one another. But these cries all relate directly to their immediate physical needs or emotional moods, and are of three kinds:

(*a*) Calls giving notice of the presence or prospect of food.

(*b*) Calls of warning in the presence or prospect of danger.

(*c*) Calls expressing feelings of joy or pain.

(*a*) and (*b*) are natural vocal responses to the

immediate physical environment, (*c*) is the expression of immediate feeling. The call to food is given by the partridge only in the presence of food; the warning cry for danger only in the presence of danger. While both, as we have said, refer to the future, it is always the near or immediate future. They stop there. The particular cry is never separated from the particular environment to which it is the natural response.]

(2) Because of the limited physical needs for which these calls are used, and because of the general vagueness of their significance, these distinguishable calls are few in number, ranging from, say, one to twelve, and these few completely answer the bird's needs. They do not increase in number. The partridge gives the same call in the presence of a dozen different kinds of food. Similarly in the case of danger. As natural sounds they are inarticulate and hence non-differentiating. When the dog barks, for example, outside the house, the bark intimates only that *something* is approaching, but leaves the human inmates of the house in doubt as to whether it is a man, horse, cow, wolf, bear, etc. The child goes to the door to ascertain what it is that is approaching and reports that it is a "man." The articulated sound "man," which he utters, explicitly differentiates the approaching object from all other possible alternatives, because "man" is not a natural sound like the "wow" of the dog, but a conventionalized sound; and it is

this articulation and conventionalization of sound, (*a*) shaping it out with clear edges to distinguish it from other sounds, and (*b*) investing it with a definite limited meaning, that makes language.

Articulate language is a composite thing; and in every word there are three distinguishable elements. (*a*) The natural sound out of which the word is made. This is the raw material of language. The animal's rudi-language stops here. (*b*) The definite shape given to this natural sound in its beginning, its middle, and its end, to separate it from other similarly shaped sounds. For example, the conventionalized sound "d-o-g" has a definite distinguishable beginning "d," a definite distinguishable tone-body "o," and a definite distinguishable ending "g," which, or any one of which, mark this sound off clearly from all other sounds. (*c*) This clearly shaped sound is invested with a definite, limited, arbitrary (or conventional) meaning. The sound "dog" stands for a particular object in nature, and is differentiated, both by its sound-shape and its conventional meaning, from its near-neighbour sound "hog" as clearly as these two objects are differentiated from each other by their space-shape in nature. In the cries of animals the two last elements of language, namely (*b*) and (*c*), are absent.

Since language is a direct product of the mind, and since the language of man differs thus clearly from the rudi-language of animals, this difference in their utterances must signify certain differences in mental powers between the two.] The language differences ought to give the clue to the mental differences if we can follow the logical deductions closely enough. If the animal does not conventionalize sound so as to differentiate one sound explicitly from another, and to multiply their number as man has done, it would seem to follow that he does not *in his mind* differentiate one object from another in space, or one event from another in time, in the explicit way that man differentiates them. Man's power of explicit mental differentiation was what brought human language into existence. For example, looking around him in any given bit of spatial environment, a man will differentiate by his eye and mind, say, fifty different objects, and will require fifty distinguishable sound symbols, concrete nouns, to differentiate them in his mental world which he elaborates by language, and which, as I shall try to show in some detail farther on, corresponds in its parts and structure to the parts and structure of the natural world he is looking at. A dog standing by his side in the same environment shows no mental urge for any such clearly defined sound symbols at all, so that he evidently does not mentally differentiate the various objects with that distinctness which creates the need of language. There is little doubt that the dog can see as man does with his physical eyes, though perhaps not so clearly, but there seems to be no *mental* recognition, and hence no *mental* interest in or curiosity about the various differentiated objects which are before his eyes. Otherwise he would be urged to the making of mental symbols to designate them as man has been urged. He seems interested in material objects in his environment only as they affect his physical needs. He sees the tree or thorn bush and avoids it; or the hole in the hedge and goes through it; and he crosses the flower bed with the same indifference as the gravel walk. He shows no mental recognition of the flower, weed, tree, hedge, stone, as objects that can be mentally differentiated. He does not see with his mind, or with a mental interest, as man does. Bring him into the master's library and he is mentally incognizant of the book, the magazine, the jug, the pipe, the chair, the ink-bottle, as things distinguished from one another physically and distinguishable mentally.

The difference is illustrated in another way by the animal's well-known habit of remaining motionless, "freezing" as it is called, to escape the notice of other animals that are within seeing distance. I stood motionless once in a quite open space for at least five minutes within twenty yards of a fox that was hunting for mice in a rotted log. There were a few stumps in the vicinity, and three times he looked at me as if curious about my identity, and eventually trotted off in a quite unconcerned manner. I should have had no difficulty in identifying the fox had he been stock-still.

That the difference between the two minds does exist is obvious from the facts of language and from other evidence similar to the instance cited here. The real difficulty is in getting the difference set out clearly enough by the mere observational method to lift it above ambiguity. To do this I shall approach the question presently by another method.

There is, however, another interesting and, as I think, legitimate comparison that might help us forward a step towards clearness in conceiving the fact of language. The articulately differentiated sounds of human speech stand to undifferentiated natural sounds in much the same relation as the explicitly differentiated bodies of the various animals stand to the undifferentiated common matter of the earth out of which the various animals' bodies have been made. All names of animals have been fashioned by man out of the common element of sound, just as all animals themselves have been fashioned by nature out of the common elements of matter. In the pre-animal stage of the world these common elements of matter were undifferentiated and formless. With the emergence of animal life individualized portions of matter took on various specific shapes and features that stand out sharply differentiated from one another in the various animals' bodies. So with language. In the pre-language stage of the world the natural sounds from which language was to be made were undifferentiated, or at most vaguely differentiated. When shaped and conventionalized by men into the names of animals these sound-names stand out as clear and distinct from one another as do the animals which they name. The world-force first differentiated common matter into distinguishable individual forms, plants, animals, birds, etc., and in this way added a new story to its life. Similarly the same world-force (whatever that force may be) working consciously in the mind of man has differentiated natural sounds into distinguishable individual names for these plants, animals, birds, etc., and in this way has again added a new story to world-life. The inconscious organized and multiform world of matter has now a duplicate in the conscious organized and multiform world of mind by means of language symbols. If the world is the veritable unity which we assert it to be, then the fabric of human language which now extends over the world of nature is as distinct a cycle in its evolution as is the cycle of animal life which extends over the surface of insentient nature. This will be made clearer a little farther on.

2. *Earth and Birds*

To most of us, a bird's a feathered song
Which for our pleasure gives a voice to spring.
We make a symbol of its airy wing
Bright with the liberty for which we long.

Or we discover them with love more strong
As each a separate individual thing
Which only learns to act or move, or sing
In ways that wholly to itself belong.

But some with deeper and more inward sight
See them a part of that one Life which streams
Slow on, towards more mind—a part more light
Than we; unburdened with regrets, or dreams,
Or thought. A winged emotion of the sky,
The birds through an eternal Present fly.

> JULIAN HUXLEY, 1934

Before passing on to the next step, the life of man,
I should like to say a few things more about the relation between animate life and the earth beneath it,
that are implied in the conception of the organic
unity of the world. The unity between the plant life
and the inorganic matter of the world is apparent to
the senses as well as to the mind. The tree is rooted
in the earth, and we can see it with our eyes as an
obvious outgrowth of the inorganic world in which its
roots remain bedded. But when we come to the animate world, the birds, for example, our senses tend
to deceive us. The robin with its body freed from
the earth appears to the sight as something moving
upon or above the earth's surface, rather than as an
outgrowth or projection of the earth. Yet the robin,
when we consider it, is obviously a projection of the
earth in the same literal sense as is the tree, and is
also, like the tree, an expression of an aspect of the

general world-life, one step in advance of the tree in the general evolution towards freedom. And there was a time in the history of the world, no doubt, when the robin's remote ancestors were not detached from the physical environment out of which they were emerging; and a point or period of time when that detachment was effected, and the great step made towards freedom. *How* the step was made is a question for the naturalist.

Similarly, when we listen to the various songs of the birds around us we are apt to think of these as merely the voices of isolated birds upon the surface of a material world. But here again if our theory of the organic nature of the world corresponds in verity to the actual nature of the world—and all our thinking leads us more and more to that view—then these voices of the birds are the voices of the world breaking through these individualized living forms which the world, in the creative evolution or unfolding of its life and mind, has by long processes produced and developed for that particular kind of utterance. In other words, the voices of the birds are the individualized and localized voices of the world; and the living impulses of joy that emanate in the bird's songs are the joy impulses of the world, as Plato pointed out long ago in *The Laws*. These songs and cries are the recently inchoate life and mind of the world emerged now into voice and expression through individualized organic bodies. What other ultimate interpretation can be given them? All recent scientific and philosophic thought, and the no less authoritative intuitive thought of poetry, when carried through to the end, leads us to this view. It is interesting to think, under the conception of emergent evolution, of the many steps and long history that lie between the original huge, formless, voiceless matter of the world in its pre-life period, and the tiny, individualized, liberated, animated piece of matter that mounts in the skylark's body and gives its portion of the world's life back to the world in song. This would be a typical example of the manner in which the world rises to its actual life and voice. The skylark, if it could speak, might well say, like Caliban's pipe in Browning's poem:

I make the cry my maker cannot make
With his great round mouth; he must blow through mine!

If it should be objected by the modern realist that the above world-view is a rather outmoded idealism at the present time, I would agree; with the rejoinder, however, that the view has persisted through many alternating fashions of philosophic thought from pre-Platonic to post-Hegelian times, and is likely to survive in modified form the present anti-idealistic mode of thought. The idealism (the word is entirely misleading to most moderns) of Hegel, for example, is not wanting in realistic content [witness his philosophy of history and of art] as the detractors of Hegel would find if they took the trouble to read his work, though he does rather ruthlessly crush the factual material in order to extract its significance. If it should be further objected that the language employed in presenting the view is the diction and phraseology of poetry rather than of sober science, the answer would be that these higher aspects of the world which we call life and mind are the aspects with which poetry is especially concerned, and that many of these aspects are so subtle, elusive, and fugitive in their nature that they cannot be caught or accurately conveyed by any diction less subtle, fluid, and accurate than the diction of poetry. And for readers who have made no close study of the exactness of poetry in dealing with its own particular phase of the truth of the world it may be worth while recalling Coleridge's observation that "poetry has a logic of its own as severe as that of science, and more difficult, because more subtle, more complex, and dependent upon more fugitive causes."

The Canadian poet Bliss Carman, in one of his poems, *The Choristers,* has given a rather striking poetic expression of the emergence of life and purposive sound in the world. He follows Plato, whether consciously or not, in conceiving mind (God) as an original element and the guiding agency in world evolution, and love and gladness as active and creative principles which in their strain and urge for expression eventually produced those tiny animated

pieces of matter, the birds, with their throats fashioned for song. Carman has used a very simple and
naïve diction, some of it, like "seraphs' chorus,"
quite archaic in comparison with modern scientific
diction, but in spite of this he has succeeded in con-
veying in a rather telling way the whole idea of the
organic unity of the world of matter-and-mind as it
emerges from lifeless to living activity.

> When earth was finished and fashioned well
> There was never a musical note to tell
> How glad God was, save the voice of the rain
> And the sea and wind on the lonely plain
> And the rivers among the hills.
> And so God made the marvellous birds
> For a choir of joy transcending words,
>
> .   .   .   .   .
>
> He filled their tiny bodies with fire,
> He taught them love for their chief desire,
>
> .   .   .   .   .
>
> And to each he apportioned a fragment of song—
> Those broken melodies that belong
> To the seraphs' chorus. . . .
>
> So music dwells in the glorious throats
> Forever, and the enchanted notes
> Fall with rapture upon our ears,
> Moving our hearts to joy and tears
> For things we cannot say.

The fact that we, the conscious recipients of these
world-voices, are so deeply and variously moved by

them, is itself the strongest kind of presumptive evidence of a causal connection, other than merely physical, between man's mind and the world-cycles of life beneath it, and also of some kind of vital purposiveness throughout the rising cycles of nature from matter to man.

This whole view is, of course, based upon the organic hypothesis described above, of a purposive activity in the world which *was working towards* the making, say, of birds before it had actually made them. When the stage was prepared and set this same purposive activity made the birds so that they could fly and sing. The length of time involved in the making, whether a thousand or a million years, does not affect the theory.

One can see no way of concretely imaging or describing this prime purposive agency, or its mode of working in the world, since, in fashioning the bird's body, it works apparently from *within* matter; while all purposive activity, which we can observe in operation now, whether in animal or in human life, imposes its purpose upon matter from *without*. I accept the purposive hypothesis because it appears the only logical one. If the parts of the bird's body were not purposively combined into a purposive organism, then they must have come together by chance. I have tried to think how particles of inorganic matter might by chance have formed themselves, in a million years, into the bones, muscles, digestive and respiratory organs, blood, flesh, skin, eyes, feathers, wings, etc., of a bird, all the parts co-ordinated and unified with the vital principle of life, and I find it absolutely impossible to imagine how it could so happen at all, any more than I can imagine particles of matter "shooting out in millions of directions for millions of years," if you like, forming themselves into a locomotive with the power of pulling a train of cars.

But this analogy, the reader may object, between the bird and the locomotive is going back again to Paley's analogy of the watch. Partly, yes. But Paley's error was not in his idea of design, or purposive activity in itself, but in his anthropomorphic conception of it. He conceived the prime creative activity as standing outside the matter of the world, and making purposive living things in much the same way as a man makes a watch. The analogy, drawn in this fashion, will not hold. The bird is a living piece of matter; the watch, lifeless. The bird seeks its own daily food, propagates its species, etc.; the watch has to be wound by man and when worn out has to be replaced by a man-made new one. The purposiveness of the watch—to mark the time—is imposed upon lifeless matter from without by external design; the purposiveness of the bird—to sing, fly, propagate, etc. —is infused into matter from within, by internal design. How so infused one sees no way of conceiving in detail at all. One merely deduces the inherence of a purposive activity in the world from the purposive nature of its products—animate nature and man. In man the purposive activity of the world comes out to complete explicitness. The entire world of art, for example, both of use and beauty, which is now spread over the world of nature on this planet is the product of explicit purpose working through the brain and hand of man, who is nature's chief product. To conceive an unbroken unity in the world one seems forced to carry the purposive activity backward down the scale of existence from the highest form, man, to its lowest form, matter.

But why, one might here ask, do I not at once call this prime vital activity in the world "God," instead of using only vague descriptive words that appear to be evading the issue? Because that would be going farther in the direction of definiteness than the formulated conception of the organic hypothesis would warrant. The word "God" connotes in the minds of most people an anthropomorphic agency, a limited personality who works towards limited particular ends, in a manner very similar to that in which human beings work. But whatever one's *belief* may be, there seems to be no way of *knowing* or *conceiving* the central creative force of the world in this definite way. The anthropomorphic conception of purpose is the highest form we *know* in the cycles of reality, and there is as yet no way of *definitely conceiving* a higher form of purposive agency who could produce purposive animated pieces of matter—birds, animals, etc.—which would be even remotely analogous to the purpose-serving inanimate machines which man can make. Since the whole hypothesis can be conceived only in a general way the diction and phraseology in which it is set out cannot legitimately be more definite than the conception in the mind.

CHAPTER VI

MAN AND THE ANIMALS

> Every animal has its sphere to which it belongs by birth, into which it instantly enters, in which it continues all through life, and in which it dies. . . . The spider weaves with as much skill as did Minerva, but all its skill is restricted to this narrow sphere; this is its universe. How marvellous is the insect and how narrow the sphere of its activity.—HERDER, *Origin of Language*, 1772.

✧ ✧ ✧ ✧

IN THE PRECEDING PAGES WE HAVE GIVEN A DESCRIPtive outline of the Space-Time picture of the life and mind of the world as it has emerged by successive steps towards freedom and individuality, up to and including animal life and intelligence. But there is as yet no language; and, from all that we can discover, no power nor problem in the animal nature which would bring language into existence. There seems to be some barrier that holds the animal's mind back from that realm of free mind into which man has entered, where language first emerges. What is the barrier? Can it be intellectually grasped and described? These are the two questions.

Darwin, as we have seen, held that there was no barrier; that the difference was merely "a difference in degree of mental development." While this state-

179

ment, as we have also seen, gives us no specific light on the problem at its present stage, it had a value in its time, and has been considered adequate by most biologists and general readers since Darwin's time, who have made no close study of language. His followers, to illustrate the view, have frequently made the statement that the difference in mental development between the lowest type of savage, the Fuegian, for example, and a fully civilized and cultivated man is greater than the difference between the same savage and the anthropoid ape. Recently I came across the following illustration, used to symbolize the relative differences.

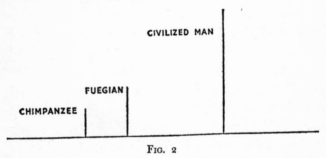

FIG. 2

But both the statement and the illustration are clearly erroneous, owing to the confusion of *resemblance* of power with *identity* of power. The error can be made very clear by an example.

If we were to take a six-month-old Fuegian infant and place him in an educated English-speaking home in Canada with its common educational opportunities, what and where would he be in twenty years? He would be first of all in complete working possession of a highly developed language, the instrument by which man has elaborated the world of mind into which he has entered and in which he realizes his characteristic destiny. Then, by means of this language, he would have elaborated concretely for himself the various parts of this mental world, in history, geography, literature, mathematics, science, and would stand in much the same position as any Canadian boy who had a long line of civilized ancestors. The seeming gulf between the savage and the civilized man would be practically bridged in a quarter of a single life-span.

Now put the chimpanzee's six-month-old offspring in the same home and environment, and at twenty years he would know none of these things. He is excluded by some impassable barrier from man's mental world, the world which man has actualized and elaborated by means of language. Darwin expresses surprise that some men should still think that there is any such barrier between the two. "Nevertheless," he writes, "many authors have insisted that man is divided by an insuperable barrier from the lower animals in his mental faculties." Well, these authors, as a matter of demonstrable fact, are right and Darwin wrong. The Fuegian is at the outset already across the barrier that stands between nature and free mind, and moves forward in that new world of free mind immediately opportunity is given. The chimpanzee is still in the world of nature, and is blocked, as yet at least, by the barrier that stands between nature and free mind, whether we can ever explicitly describe that barrier or not. The savage is, as it were, just across the barrier into the new world, while the civilized man has gone a great way inland, so that the savage in his outward appearance more closely resembles his nearest of kin in the old world which he has just left than he does his actual brother who has gone so far ahead of him in the new world. But whatever *resemblances* there may be in mental faculty between the chimpanzee and the savage, it is clearly a *resemblance* merely and not an *identity* of power.

That Darwin and his followers should have fallen into and persisted in this now obvious confusion regarding the respective mental powers of the animals and man is a striking illustration of how even the most careful scientist may fall a prey to unscientific prejudices against old forms of thought and their mode of expression; and how these prejudices, coupled with his desire for complete coherence in the new thought which he is elaborating, may blind him to significant facts in the old quite as completely as any popular or theological prejudice can blind its adherents to the truth of the new. When, for example, the old writer on the Genesis of life in the world represented man's fall (or awakening) from innocence as resulting from his eating of a forbidden fruit, and the consequent opening of his eyes to a knowledge of good and evil, truth and error, etc., leading in turn to his expulsion from the Garden of Eden (the world of nature, in modern colourless phraseology), and his giving names to the things in the natural world, he gave one of the most memorable accounts that will ever be given of one of the most momentous facts in the story of emergent evolution of life and mind in the world. When the novelty of recent discoveries has worn off a little, and the mind of the modern world, settled into something of a sober perspective again, returns with a more flexible intelligence to a reading of that old story, it will perhaps wonder that an allegory which so vividly images forth a cardinal fact in world history should have fallen into even temporary disrepute through the obloquy thrown upon it by the prejudice of novel discoveries, however important these discoveries themselves may turn out to be. Every new truth, however, must at first make its way against the jealous prejudices of the old, and by the very spirit of aggression necessary to expel the old the new truth is apt to develop its own prejudice in the manner of a defensive armour. It requires only a little heat in the mind to smudge the features of the fairest truth with its affined prejudice.

CHAPTER VII

THE BARRIER OF SPACE
AND TIME

Space and Time as infinite and all-embracing wholes are *a priori* intuitions which are the condition of and antecedent to all our knowledge of particular objects in space and time.—KANT, *Critique of Pure Reason,* 1781.

⟡　　⟡　　⟡　　⟡

WHAT, THEN, IS THE BARRIER BETWEEN THE ANImals and man, that excludes the animals from man's mental world? It is the barrier primarily of Space and Time. This, I think, can be made clear.

First, consider Time. It is clear, to begin with, that the dog holds in his memory, at least in some dim way, the time-span, or the time experiences, within the physical duration of his own life. The dog will go to-day where he found food yesterday. Darwin's dog recognized him after an absence of five years and two days. Odysseus's dog, Argus, according to Homer, recognized his master, even through his beggar's disguise, after an absence of twenty years. There is no doubt that the dog has memory of this kind, which shows that he has some grasp of time within his own life-span. Whether it is conscious memory with an explicit measurement of a stretch of time between a point in past time and the present moment, as is the case with man's memory, is extremely doubtful. It seems to be rather a recognition of the master's identity, or sameness, through a succession of experiences, each of which is for the dog a present experience without any explicit differentiation of time into past and present.

Because—and this is the vital point—while it is clear that the dog has some kind of memory, and hence some grasp of time within his own physical life-span, it is equally clear, so far as can be discovered, that the dog has no sense of time prior to his own birth or subsequent to his own death. He has no sense or consciousness of any dog's life of a hundred years ago. He could not be awakened to any consciousness of or interest in the story of Darwin's dog, nor could Darwin's dog have been awakened to an interest in the dog of Odysseus. The time before and after his own actual life-span is as completely hidden from him as the past and future were hidden from the passengers over Mirza's bridge by the impenetrable mists that hung at either end. His mind is enveloped and confined by time within the short span of his own physical life.

Man's mind, on the other hand, though centred in a material body like the dog's, has broken through this envelope or sense-barrier of time, and holds all time now in its grasp instead of being held by it. It has no more difficulty in holding Homer's story of three thousand years ago than Darwin's of a hundred years ago, and it explicitly differentiates the stretch of time between the two events. To all this past time the dog's mind is stone-dead. To object that the dog has no language for the differentiation of time into explicit parts is to reverse the true logic, because language is just the instrument created by man to actualize and elaborate his new world of Free Mind into which he had emerged, and of which time is one of the forms; and the dog whose mind is unfreed and still encompassed in time has no such time-world of mind to elaborate, and hence no language or need of language. In other words man's mind has broken through the sense-limiting medium of time, has encompassed time in its grasp, and now holds all time in its single view as the potential form in which to build up and arrange a mental world of succession and development. Language is the system of symbols created to elaborate this new world.

The same difference is true of Space. The dog has some kind of mental knowledge of that local portion of space in which his body moves about, the space which lies within the range of his senses and experience, but he never breaks through the circle of that limited range to the grasp of space as a whole. While he remains in Vancouver his mind cannot be awakened to any sense or consciousness of a dog show in Montreal, three-thousand-odd miles away. His mind, though radiating to a certain circumference beyond his body, is nevertheless enclosed, like his body, within a local space as we found it enclosed within a local time. To the dog's master, on the other hand, the dog show three thousand miles away is as mentally present while he reads of it on the news page of his evening paper as the dog show two blocks away in his own town, which he reads of also on the same page. Distance or nearness in actual space makes no difference mentally at all, since all points are merely differentiations of a single space which he holds within his mind as an always-present mental world.

It is true that man never actually *perceives* space and time in their entirety with his senses. The range of his physical sight has apparently the same physical limitations as the range of the animal's. But his mental differentiation of objects within his local space-time environment is so complete and explicit that the mind has no difficulty in visualizing limitless stretches of space and time beyond the range of the senses. A small map of the world's surface, for example, of a single square foot in dimension, which he looks at with his eyes, is only a miniature material picture of the mental picture which he visualizes in his mind, and whose actual physical dimensions extend to thousands of square miles, far beyond the range of his senses.

This is the unique characteristic of the human mind. In each isolated piece of matter of some two and three-quarter cubic feet and one hundred and seventy-five pounds avoirdupois, which makes up a man's body, there is centred a power which radiates to the farthest boundaries of space and time. Even the behaviourist who attempts to explain all actions of the mind on a physical basis of stimulus and response will admit this. (See J. B. Watson, *Behaviorism,* 1930, Chap. X on "Talking and Thinking.")

It is very probable, though one sees no way as yet of actually demonstrating it, that the animal's mental inability to differentiate objects explicitly within his local environment, which we have referred to above, is due to the fact that his mind does not hold space and time explicitly within its grasp as does man's mind. Kant held, and in fact made it quite clear, that man's mental possession of space and time as wholes preceded the explicit differentiation of local objects in a limited portion of space and time, and so, in the *Transcendental Aesthetic,* he enunciated the doctrine that space and time are forms of the mind, and not external to it, as they appear to the senses to be. This was perhaps his most significant original contribution to the whole problem of mind, though, as pointed out in the beginning, we have not yet made full use of it.

This sense and grasp of space and time as wholes, with the consequent explicit differentiation of objects within any local portion of space and time, is perhaps the significant part of the concrete definition of

consciousness in man as distinguished from the inconscious mind of animals. The clearest single statement I know of this difference comes from Browning. In his discussion of the problem of human happiness in *Cleon,* he has, in a memorable passage of
twenty-eight lines, made one of the most determined
and successful attempts to set out clearly the nature
of this special quality or power in the human mind
which distinguishes man from the animals. Though
written in verse it is expressed with unique precision,
and is intended to be read with the same literalness as
the most exact scientific prose. The passage is sup-
posedly written by a Greek philosopher-poet, Cleon,
in a letter to his king and patron, Protus.

If, in the morning of philosophy,
Ere aught had been recorded, nay perceived,
Thou, with the light now in thee, couldst have looked
On all earth's tenantry, from worm to bird,
Ere man, her last, appeared upon the stage—
Thou wouldst have seen them perfect, and deduced
The perfectness of others yet unseen.
Conceding which—had Zeus then questioned thee
"Shall I go on a step, improve on this,
Do more for visible creatures than is done?"
Thou wouldst have answered, *"Ay, by making each
Grow conscious in himself*—by that alone.
All's perfect else: the shell sucks fast the rock,
The fish strikes through the sea, the snake both swims
And slides, forth range the beasts, the birds take flight,
Till life's mechanics can no further go—
And all this joy in natural life is put

Like fire from off thy finger into each,
So exquisitely perfect is the same.
But 'tis pure fire, and they mere matter are:
It has them, not they it; and so I choose
For man, thy last premeditated work
(If I might add a glory to the scheme),
That a third thing should stand apart from both,
A quality arise within his soul,
Which, intro-active, made to supervise
And feel the force it has, may view itself,
And so be happy."

It would be difficult to make a clearer or more precise statement in prose of the difference in mental fact between the animals and man, though Browning has stated the difference in relation to conduct and happiness while we are investigating the difference in relation to knowledge.

Following out our argument from the point of view of space and time, let us attempt to put the significant difference between the two into a concise statement. The animal's mind, like his body, is held within the sense limits of space and time; but man's mind, though focused in the body, has broken completely through both these forms and now holds both time and space within itself. Or more succinctly still, time-and-space holds the animal's mind; man's mind holds time-and-space. The difference is fundamental, and, in the things that follow from it, is as significant as any difference we know in the scale of emergent organic life in the world. The whole point made here is only, as already pointed out, the logical extension and concrete application of Kant's view in the *Transcendental Aesthetic of Pure Reason* where he showed that space and time are forms of the mind and not external to it, though Kant might not hold his doctrine responsible for all that seems to me to follow from it. It would all be implied, however, in Hegel's development of Kant's doctrine, if I do not misunderstand Hegel.

This rising above space and time, and enclosing them within his own ubiquitous and omnipresent self, "a universal here and now," seems to be the basic difference between man and the animals in their mental powers, when considered in their objective characteristics and behaviour. Other differences follow naturally upon this one, since time and space are the forms within which the whole world is constructed. While a man, for example, sits within the walls of his own study, 14 ft. by 12 ft. by 10 ft. in its actual physical dimensions, and goes over the world-news page of his daily paper, he reads one item from England, another from Greece, another from Russia, another from Japan, another from his own town; one item from to-day, another of five years ago, another of five hundred years ago, another of five thousand; but these various items, scattered through leagues and years of actual space and time, are all equally present, and within his mental possession, while his body sits at home here and now in his own study. All these differentiated items which are obviously *outside* his own body in space and time are just as obviously —when we think closely about it—and in the same literal sense *within* his mind. When, for example, we make distinction in time, say between 450 B.C. and A.D. 450, we are making distinctions within the mind, not outside of it. That is, the mind, though focused and centred in a body in this present time and space, holds all time and space within itself. It is itself in a quite literal sense co-terminous with space and time. When the poet wrote:

> Backward, turn backward, O Time, in thy flight,
> Make me a child again just for to-night,

he could not have expressed the longing for the physical return of childhood did he not hold in his mind as a present possession the mental counterpart of it. It is the contrast between the mental presence of the past time and the absence of its physical counterpart that makes the point in the song.

It is difficult to realize actually this limitless range of the human mind because the evidence from our senses is all against it. We see our bodies and the bodies of one another as local objects like any other objects confined always to a particular time and space, and to say that the mind, which comes to a focus of consciousness in this same body, is not so confined but free of both time and space, or rather holds time and space within itself, sounds like a fine flourish of rhetoric rather than a plain statement of fact. Fact it is, nevertheless; the fact which separates man from his animal relatives, and which necessitates articulate language for man while the animals remain without it. Whether we call this a difference of degree or kind is a matter of agreement on the connotations of terms. The two words, however, as already pointed out, have served their day and their inherent vagueness renders them quite useless in any precise modern discussion of the subject.

CHAPTER VIII

MAN

The termination of the world in a man appears to be the last victory of intelligence. . . . The great Pan of old, who was clothed in a leopard-skin to signify the beautiful variety of things, and the firmament, his coat of stars—was but the representative of thee, O rich and various Man! thou palace of sight and sound, carrying in thy senses the morning and the night and the unfathomable galaxy; in thy brain, the geometry of the City of God; in thy heart, the bower of love and the realms of right and wrong. An individual man is a fruit which it cost all the foregoing ages to form and ripen. . . . Each individual soul is such, in virtue of its being a power to translate the world into some particular language of its own.—EMERSON, *The Method of Nature.*

❖   ❖   ❖   ❖

1. *The Emergence of Consciousness*

IF WE NOW RELATE THIS UNIQUE CHARACTERISTIC OF man in a definite and explicit way with the general Time-and-Space picture which we have been drawing, we shall see plainly the full significance of this last step—where mind in man emerges to freedom from space and time, and encompasses them in its grasp—in the unfolding life and mind of the world.

Recall again our working hypothesis, the organic unity of the world from matter to man. For aeons, if science speaks truly, our earth, to human perception at least, stood stark and naked, a mineral mass. In the process of time this seeming mineral mass clothed itself in life, in sensitivity, in mind. These later emergents, if the world is, as science asserts, an organic whole, are not adventitious decorations like tinsel on a Christmas tree, nor alien visitants extraneous to reality. They are the children of the earth who owe to her creating and shaping energy their multivarious forms and powers, physical and mental, and derive from her directly and indirectly their hourly nourishment, all without design on their own part. Life and mind which have emerged to explicit activity in these later cycles of world evolution must have been present as latent potentialities when the earth seemed but a mineral mass; and purpose, which is the explicit directing agency in all man's activity, must have been, as it seems to us, the prime directing agency of the whole evolutionary process, though emerging to explicitness first in animal nature, especially man. How otherwise, for example, could the human organism, when the hour for its awakening into consciousness came, find all its numerous and minutest parts so finely co-ordinated and articulated into a purposive agent for explicit design and execution?

We deduce the purposiveness of the entire evolutionary process from base to peak from the fact that purposiveness explicitly emerges to view at the peak, and all the earlier or lower stages seem to be adapted

in an anticipatory way to produce these purposive
agents at the top and to co-ordinate their inward and
outward environment with a view to their successful
purposive activities. If this hypothesis be right, then
the purposive shaping principle at work in the world
seems to have worked for an indefinite period of its
history in an embryonic fashion from within, in the
dark as it were, among the sensuous materials of the
world, fashioning and moulding these materials into
the forms necessary for the actualization of its own
emerging life, but all the while mute and unconscious
of the process. First, the many differentiated inorganic
structures, then upward into the organic world
through an ascending series of insentient and sentient
life, rising in each step to a higher freedom and a
more self-contained individuality. Then, as a last and
crowning step—so far at least as the earth goes at
the present time—this purposive shaping principle
produces the adequate individual organism man,
by means of which she emerges above the sense media
of space and time, encompasses and holds these
within her view, awakens to freedom and consciousness and, turning back, as it were, upon herself, is
confronted with the endlessly diversified forms of all
her own preconscious evolution. Man is nature at the
highest point of her activity; and when we speak, in
our ordinary dualistic way, of man investigating
nature in knowledge, we mean, if we are thinking
philosophically at all, that nature, emerging into self-

consciousness at her apex in man, is now busy exploring from that peak the lower cycles of her own
nature. We can visualize the whole picture more
clearly, perhaps, through a simple symbolic diagram
than through a written description.

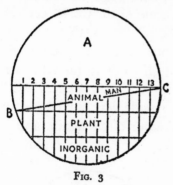

Fig. 3

Let the circle A represent the actualized world up
to that point where reason emerges to consciousness
in man, and the three zones represent the cycles of
inorganic, plant, and animal life, respectively. Let
the vertical lines represent the successive generations
of plant and animal life as they pass through the
world, and the rising line BC represent the general
evolutionary time-line of man's life in the world up
to the point C where he emerges to consciousness.
Previous to the point C in the evolution time-line the
world was a single space-time world whose individualized forms were differentiated and distributed in
space, and moved forward as an ever-vanishing series
in time. All its objects were encompassed in space

and enveloped in time. The generation of animals which were alive, for example, between lines 10 and 11 had no sense of time previous to 10, nor subsequent to 11, as we have already shown.

But at the point C where man emerged to consciousness the mind of the world, centered now in the human organism, broke through the enveloping mediums of both space and time, and encompassed these within itself so as to hold the whole world of space and time within its single view. This new expansion can be made very clear by a further illustration. If we take our circle again, and remember the rising line BC symbolizes the evolutionary time-line

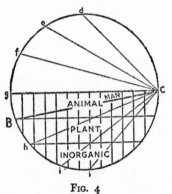

Fig. 4

of man's ancestry, up to the point C, where world consciousness emerges in man, then this emergence to consciousness where the world turns back upon itself and encompasses itself in a single view (unactualized, of course, at this point, but real) would be accurately symbolized by the lighter lines radiating from C backwards, C-d, C-e, C-f, etc., over the whole space-time world.

Now we have in a quite literal sense two worlds of space and time: the *actual* space-time world of material nature represented by the horizontal and vertical lines, and the *ideal* space-time world of mind represented by the lines radiating outward from C; and the two worlds are co-terminous.

2. *A Duplicate World*

Soon the human has a verbal substitute within himself theoretically for every object in the world. *Thereafter he carries the world around with him by means of this organization.* And he can manipulate this world in the privacy of his room or when he lies down on his bed in the dark.—J. B. WATSON, *Behaviorism,* revised edition, 1930, p. 234.

This new mental space-time world which emerges at C in conscious reason is a duplicate or counterpart of the actual space-time world of sense, so that the world which was formerly a single sensuous world now becomes a dual world. On the one hand there is the material space-time world of sensuous nature already highly actualized in all sorts of inorganic and organic forms. Previous to the emergence of conscious reason in man this was the single and only actualized world. Now, on the other hand, there emerges the mental space-time world of conscious reason, individualized and focused in the brain of man, and confronted in this its birth hour with that other already elaborated space-time world of nature. This new (inward) mental space-time world which radiates from its centre in man's physical organism stands as the awakened counterpart of the actualized natural world. This mental world, as I am describing it here, corresponds, as said above, to Kant's exposition of space and time where he showed that these are forms of the mind—"an *ideal* space and time," as he called it—that make possible our experience of objects that appear external to one another in space, and in succession in time. All our experience of the world arranges itself in these two media. I am assuming, however—what Kant of course did not assume, and what may at first appear from a philosophic point of view a rather naïve assumption—that there is a real or sensuous space-time world in which physical objects actually exist independent of the perceiving mind, and which was already highly actualized before the birth of free and conscious mind with its ideal space-and-time that came into being with it. This ideal, non-sensuous, mental space-time world is, as I have said, the conscious duplicate or counterpart of the real, sensuous, material, "inconscious" space-time world of nature.

To illustrate concretely from common experience. If when planning a journey I should take an ordinary map, eight by ten inches in size, of those parts of the world which I plan to visit, that map would be an objective physical miniature of the ideal space-time world which I hold in my mind. Under the guidance of this ideal space-time world which I hold in my mind I would locate on the miniature physical map before me Algiers, Naples, Athens, Rome, Paris, London; calculate, again with the guidance of the ideal world of my mind, the number of actual miles of space and hours of time that lay between me and each of these places in turn, and in this way, in half an hour of actual time, I should map out in the ideal space-time world of my own mind the entire journey which would afterwards require two months of actual time for physical actualization in the actual space-time world of nature. In that condensed time of half an hour the journey would be completely visualized in the mental space-time world. Next morning I would set out physically to make the journey in the actual space-time world, and would travel mile by mile the five-thousand-odd miles in actual space in two months of actual time. The point is that the space-time world of mind which I traversed while my body sat for half an hour in a single point in actual space in my study, is the mental counterpart of the actual space-time world which I traversed afterwards in two months of actual time. With the birth of conscious reason, as stated above, a second world emerges as the conscious counterpart of the first, so that now we have a dual world.

3. *The New Problem of Conscious Reason*

Plants are evidently for the sake of animals and animals for the sake of man; thus Nature, which does nothing in vain, has done all things for the sake of man, who is the crowning end, purpose, or final cause towards which all has been tending.—ARISTOTLE.

Round his mysterious Me, there lies, under all those wool-rags, a Garment of Flesh (or of Senses), contextured in the Loom of Heaven; whereby he is revealed to his like, and dwells with them in UNION and DIVISION; and sees and fashions for himself a Universe, with azure Starry Spaces, and long Thousands of Years. . . . Stands he not thereby in the centre of Immensities, in the conflux of Eternities?—CARLYLE, *Sartor Resartus,* "Pure Reason."

But man's new mental space-time world of conscious reason is in this its birth-hour a mere potential world without concrete filling or content; an empty world. The world of sensuous nature, on the other hand, its outward counterpart, is already, in its own right, as we might put it, a highly differentiated and organized world, an actual cosmos. The new phenomenon may again be made visually clear by reverting to our former diagram.

Letting circle A again represent first the actual world of nature, the horizontal lines marking the zones of inorganic and organic forms in the world, the vertical lines marking their succession in time, the rising line BC the evolutionary time processes to the point C where conscious reason emerges, and the lighter lines radiating from C backwards marking the new space-time world of conscious mind as it radiates outward over the natural world as its conscious counterpart.

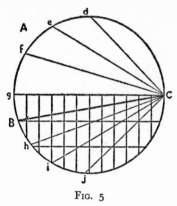

Fig. 5

Now if in imagination we turn this space-time world of mind off the space-time world of nature so that we can see, as it were, in its own nature, we shall have Fig. 6, which would be a fairly accurate symbolic representation of the situation at the dawn of conscious reason at C. Here the circle A_1 marks the space-time world of nature already highly actualized; A_2 the new space-time world of mind just born and entirely empty.

The task set to man, then, on emerging into possession of this new world of conscious mind, was to "intellect" the world, to take mental possession of it, to transfer its types one by one from the outward space-time world of nature to the inner space-time world of mind, and to build them up into a conscious system there in correspondence to this actual outward system in external nature. Or to restate the situation

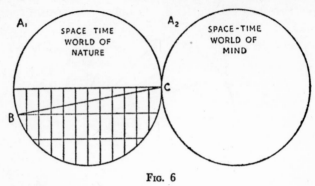

Fig. 6

from the evolution point of view, in the awakened reason of man the world emerges into a new cycle of its rising life, splits into two halves, an outer and an inner, passes from inconscious to conscious activity, and man emerges as the world-born conscious organism to bring to actualization this new cycle of world development. Or in still more vitally organic phrase, new-born man *is* the world at that point where its reason comes to a focus, emerges to consciousness, turns back upon itself, and is confronted with the task of taking conscious possession of itself by translating its actual physical types into their mental counterparts, of exploring all the steps and stages of its preconscious evolution.

In this step, however, across the boundary from nature into free mind, from the sensuous world to its supra-sensuous counterpart, a problem rises that is new in the world. How can man, just come into possession of his new conscious world, actually get started upon the task to which he is called: the task of translating the actualized space-time world of nature into the new-born space-time world of mind? His consciousness in this its birth-hour is a mere potential, and as yet quite empty world. What are the *means* then, or the media, by which he can build up within his empty reason an actual and organized structure of differentiated forms, images, and ideas, that will reflect in that inner ideal world the ordered outward system of the actual world? That is the world problem that emerges at this point in its evolution. It is an entirely new problem. There is no such problem for the animals in the cycle of nature beneath man.

CHAPTER IX

LANGUAGE

Nature gives no power in vain. She not only gave to man the power to invent language, but made the power his specific characteristic and the dynamic principle of his destiny. This power came from her hand as a living principle. . . . Reason was incapable of action without a word-symbol, and the first moment of rationality must also have been the first beginning of interior language. . . . Man feels with his mind and speaks while he thinks; therefore, the development of language is as natural to man as his nature.—HERDER, *The Origin of Language,* 1772.

❖   ❖   ❖   ❖

1. *The Birth of Language*

OBVIOUSLY, WHAT MAN REQUIRED WAS A SYSTEM OF mental symbols of some kind or other in the inner world of mind, to represent the system of actual types in the outward world of sense. Each species or type of object in the outward world of nature would require its corresponding symbol in the inward world of mind. Without such mental symbols no articulated advance could be made in that process which we now speak of familiarly as the accumulation of the knowledge of the world. The advance could be made only step by step, and each step would have to be recorded, registered, and fixed by means of its symbol within the rising mental fabric. The discovery or creation of adequate symbols of reason, then, was an obvious necessity for man even to get definitely started at all upon the elaboration or actualization of the world of mind.

It was out of this necessity that the articulate and cumulative language of man had its birth. Language is just that needed system of symbols which man has created for the elaboration of that new space-time world of mind to which he was called by the "World-Spirit" when the world emerged from the preconscious to the conscious cycle of its self-development.

Language, then, is a new phenomenon in the world, brought into life at that point where the reason of the world emerges from its inconscious state to its freed and conscious life. There is always a difficulty in coming to a mutual understanding upon the connotation of words; but it becomes palpably clear when the subject is developed in this way that to call the natural cries of animals language, without some specific qualification of the word, is a sheer confusion of all significant differences in reality and thought. The animals, as yet as least, have no free space-time world of mind whose detailed elaboration necessitates the symbols which we call language, and until they have such a world they can have no language in any exact connotation of the word.

2. *Characteristics of the New World of Language*

> But the Intellect can raise,
> From airy words alone, a Pile that ne'er decays.
> WORDSWORTH, *Inscription at Coleorton*, 1811.

To come to a clear and exact understanding of the nature of the new symbols which were required to elaborate the new world of mind, it will be necessary to point out the significant characteristics of this new mental world as distinguished from the natural world.

(1) This new world of conscious mind is, first of all, not a mere addition or expansion of the sensuous world of nature. In its elaboration there is nothing added to the sum-total of the natural material world.

(2) Nor is it any mere modification of the natural world. It involves no changes in that world. It is, on the contrary, a new and distinct world now come for the first time into actual existence, an invisible supra-sensuous world rising above and as a counterpart of the visible sensuous world.

(3) The natural world is in constant process of change, a perpetual flux, as Heraclitus observed, a vanishing world whose specific forms are continuously passing away. The mental or spiritual world, on the other hand, rises with a cumulative movement into a fixed, non-vanishing structure. It is St. Paul's contrast, if you like, between the visible and invisible worlds, the "temporal" and the "eternal," if we shift the contrast from the realm of conduct to the realm

of knowledge. One is fleeting, the other enduring. From the myriad forms of nature that are continually coming into being and passing away, conscious reason extracts one by one, as we might put it, the permanent types, and attaches each to a permanent symbol, and in this way builds up in its own inward world a structure of images and ideas that reflects the natural world and approximates more and more towards a complete counterpart of it. History, for example, as it stands actualized at the present moment in books, is the extracted and gathered-up transcript of a past, and now vanished, series of sense-events in time; and the non-sensuous, non-vanishing symbols of language have accomplished the task. *Language introduced the element of permanence into a vanishing world.* A symbolic diagram will make the point clear, though it will only repeat in a visualized form what we have already said in words.

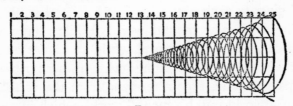

FIG. 7

Let five horizontal lines represent roughly five classes of organic life in their vanishing series in time; and an indefinite number of vertical lines mark the successive generations in this vanishing time-series; and the vertical line 13 represent the point where

conscious reason emerged in man. Then previous to
the point at 13 there was no consciousness of past or
future beyond the birth and death dates of any living
organism. The whole world could be described as a
constantly vanishing one, whose passing generations
could be truly represented by the clear-dividing vertical lines. An animal born at 7 and dying at 8 had
no outlook in time on either side beyond these limits.
Time confined him to this short interval of his own
life-span.

But with the emergence to consciousness at 13 the
envelope of time is penetrated before and after. Both
time and space are now encompassed in a single view.
Instead of encompassing they are encompassed. A
mental world emerges into being. Man looks abroad
from his physical life-centre upon the objects of the
natural world which are now encompassed in his
mental view, differentiates them from one another,
and gives to each natural object a mental symbol to
fix it in his new mental world. While man in his
physical life in the natural world continues as formerly in the vanishing time series, he transcribes, as
he passes along, type after type from the vanishing
natural world into his mental world, which increases
in content and dimensions, and does not pass away,
so that this rising world can no longer be represented
by vertical lines dividing the vanishing generations
from each other, but by an increasing spiral movement representing movement and permanence as

illustrated in Fig. 7. In this single diagram, then, we can see quite clearly the permanence of the world of mind as it rises above and in contrast with the vanishing world of sense. There is no such actualized and articulated world of mind in animal nature. The spiral diagram represents a new cycle in the evolution of the world.

3. Required Characteristics of Language

> And books are yours
> Within whose silent chambers treasure lies
> Preserved from age to age.
> WORDSWORTH, *The Excursion*, Book IV, 1814.

These, then, are the significant characteristics of the world of free mind which man is called on to elaborate, and the symbols of language required for its elaboration must correspond to it in their nature. Hence these language symbols must be:

(1) Supra-sensuous in import. I say "in import" because both *sound* and *form*, the body of oral and written language respectively, are made from sensuous elements.

(2) They must be fluid and cumulative on the one hand, and at the same time fixed and permanent, since this is the double nature of the mental world.

(3) They must be explicitly differentiated from one another, both in form and meaning, as the types

of the world which they translate are explicitly differentiated from one another.

(4) They must be representative of both space and time, since they are to translate a world which is actualized in space and time.

(5) They must be in a real sense, and by some means or other, freed from the sense limits of space and time as conscious mind is free. They must, in other words, be liberated from the vanishing nature of time, and from the rigid fixity of space, since the mind holds both motion and permanence, time and space, in a constant union. Where could such symbols be found?

4. *The Raw Material of Language*

For strangely in this so solid-seeming World, which nevertheless is in continual restless flux, it is appointed that *Sound,* to appearance the most fleeting, should be the most continuing of all things.—CARLYLE, *Sartor Resartus,* "Pause," 1830.

It is obvious that the symbols for language could not be obtained ready-made from the world of nature from which man had just emerged, for everything here is in space and time and subject to all their conditions. Nor could they be found in the new world of conscious mind into which he had just emerged because this was as yet a mere potential and quite empty world. A third alternative remained. The raw material for the symbols had to be obtained from the space-and-time-bound world of nature, since there was no other source. "Man," said Herder, "cannot invent, but only find and imitate." Awakened reason, therefore, had first to discover the adequate sensuous raw material for language from the natural world, and then had to transmute it in some way into free supra-sensuous symbols in correspondence with its own nature. The discovery of the adequate sensuous material in the actual space-time world of nature, and the transmutation of this raw material into the adequate supra-sensuous symbols of the newly emerged space-time world of mind, was the unique task and the unique achievement of conscious mind in man. It was the bridge to its new freedom, the key and instrument for the elaboration of its new world. The awakening of conscious reason in man, and the invention of these supra-sensuous symbols in the form of connotative language for the actualization of its new life, mark, as we have said, the emergence of a new phenomenon in the evolution of the world. To confuse this, by our modern prejudice for some abstract unity of the world, with any rudimentary resemblances of it in the animal world, is to obscure a unique and fundamental difference in the ascending scale of existence.

Where, then, in the sensuous world of nature was man to find the adequate raw material for language?

In nature, multitudinous as her forms are, there are only two fundamental generic types, corresponding to the two sense media, space and time. *Form,* or shape, is the natural expression of space; *sound* is the natural and direct expression of time. On the passive side the eye is the receiving organ of the expressions of space, the ear of the expressions of time.

And now the question: Which of these two, the space-forms of *shape* or the time-forms of *sound,* was to prove the natural raw material of language? Experience has already answered the question, so far as the fact is concerned. All tribes and all nations of men on the earth have made their language out of *sound.* What is left us here, then, is to discover the logical reason for the fact.

Why has man universally used sound-speech addressing itself to the ear rather than pictorial or gesture-speech addressing itself to the eye? Darwin, in his discussion of the question, has given a very concise summary of the reasons put forward for this fact. (1) While the hands were employed in gestural speech they could not be used for other necessary work. With vocal speech the hands are left free. (2) Oral speech is a more universal medium of communication. It can be heard in the dark, or on the other side of a wall, or while the person's back is turned; while sign-speech requires light for the eye to see, and can only be received when the eye is turned in that direction and no object intervenes. (3) Sound radiates from the speaker in every direction in a way that gesture-speech does not.

There are, however, other limitations of gesture-speech which are more fundamental than those enumerated above. If each gesture stood for an idea, or a word as we now have it, we should require as many gestures as there are ideas. But such a vast and ever-increasing multitude of distinguishable gestures of spatial shapes could not be made with the hands. Nor is there any way by which whole gestures, each representing an idea as a word does at the present time, could be broken up into elements as has been done with written sound-speech in the alphabet. Distinguishable gestures are each an unanalyzable whole. The deaf-mute, of course, can be taught to represent the twenty-six sound elements of the modern English alphabet by twenty-six shapings of the fingers and hands, but each of these sound elements is represented by a complete gesture, and not by the element of a gesture; and for deaf-mutes we never could have thought of reducing a gesture language to twenty-six elements had not an artificial clue been given from the twenty-six already differentiated elements of sound-language. (I am arbitrarily using the number twenty-six merely because that is the number of letters in our own English alphabet.) Even when we have devised a gesture language of twenty-six elements by twenty-six finger and hand formations, each word in conversation has to be spelled out by the separate letter-gestures, if we use alphabetic elements, while in oral speech we have to utter only single synthetic sounds where each sound includes an indefinite number of alphabetical elements, as, for example, in the word "crash," where the whole synthetic sound "crash" can be uttered as easily and in practically as short a time as can any one of its five separate alphabetic elements.

The sound-speech, on the other hand, was capable of being broken up into elements because of the original nature of the vocal organs. These organs were shaped so as to produce, first of all, say, five distinguishable basic tones, a, e, i, o, u (I am using the arbitrary number *five* because that is the number of our actual written vowel-symbols in English), and then to modify these tones in twenty-one distinguishable ways in their beginning, or ending, or sometimes in their continuance, by the lips, tongue, teeth, and nose, as represented now by the consonants b, c, d, f, g, etc. Now each one of these distinguishable tones, as also the distinguishable modifications in their beginnings, continuance, or endings, were separable within the composite word-sound, as, for example, b-a-d, though in oral speech we do not explicitly separate them. The enormous advantage of this analysis into elements for the purpose of converting sound-speech into visual speech is apparent at once, since the whole thing can be done by twenty-six spatial symbols. From the nature of the hands no such

simplification of gesture-speech would have been possible. In fact, it is quite impossible to think of any
way in which anything like a sufficient number of
distinguishable gestures could have been made to
satisfy the requirements of language at all, had not
vocal language given us the key to the method.

But all these, important as they may be, are from
a logical point of view secondary reasons why sound
was chosen rather than gestures as the substance of
human speech. The primary logical reason for the
use of sound as the material of speech is that the
process of translating the world from nature into
mind is a *time process,* it all passes through the logic
of thinking; and sound being the natural expression
of time becomes, *ipso facto,* the direct and instinctive
expression of the thought process. Thinking being a
time process, a generating of a new world, and sound
a time expression, thought and oral expression become merely the inward and outward sides of a single
time-movement. Modern psychology seems to be coming more and more to the view that the brain movements in thinking, and the movements of the vocal
organs in speech, are inseparably connected, the one
being the outward expression of the other. This is
further evidence of the teleological co-ordination of
man's physiological structure prior to the actual emergence of language. Primitive man everywhere apparently felt the causal connection between the two, and
acted on the impulse of his feeling in using sound in

his very first steps in language. Even in silent thinking we are conscious of a corresponding movement by the vocal organs when we attend to it, though no audible sound issues from the lips. It might, of course, be countered here that this connection between thinking and the vocal organs may be due to long and close association of the two. The evidence, however, seems to point to a more fundamental connection.

5. *The Dual Power of Language through Conventionalization of Natural Sounds*

. . . manifesting one's thought by the voice with *nouns* and *verbs,* imaging the opinion of the mind in the stream which flows from the lips, as in a mirror.—PLATO, *Theaetetus,* 206.

And now we come to a unique phase of the problem, and one that, so far as I know, has been overlooked up to the present time. Natural sound can translate or express pure time only. It cannot, except in the vaguest kind of way, translate or express to the mind objects or forms in space. Instrumental music, as a pure time art built up of natural sound, illustrates the point clearly. In fact, one characteristic of pure time as expressed directly by natural sound is its indefiniteness. It is space, and objects in space, that give objective definiteness to our world; though time, when expressed indirectly by movement or change of position of objects in space, takes on a certain bor-

rowed definiteness from the objects concerned, and
from their characteristic movements. But pure time
as expressed by natural sound can have no objective
definiteness at all.

Now the question: How can sound, which in its
natural form can express time only, and addresses
itself to the ear, be made to translate a world of spatial objects as well, which are clearly differentiated
from one another, and address themselves to the eye?
This could be done only by the *conventionalization*
of natural sounds, by transmuting *sounds* into *sound
symbols,* so that while the natural sensuous sound
element still remains, as it must, a time expression,
the conventionalized sound symbol into which it is
converted may express either time or space. This
is what has actually been done in every human
language. For example, in the expression "The dog
barks," the conventionalized sound "dog," though
conveyed by sound to the ear, expresses a space form,
i.e. it raises a spatial image in the mind; while the
conventionalized sound "barks" conveys a time expression. Both of these words have the common sensuous element of sound as their raw material, and
each requires a certain duration of time for its expression, as all sound does; but by definite shaping of this
raw sound material, and by investing the definite
shape with a definite arbitrary or conventional meaning, the two sounds have been differentiated so as to
express space and time with equal facility. In lan-

guage, then, as we have it in human speech, the natural sound element has been taken up into and practically disappears from our consciousness in its significant symbolic connotation. In other words, the natural sounds have been completely transmuted into conventional sound-symbols. This is what constitutes language, and has enabled man to elaborate a complete space-time world of mind which rises above the space-time world of nature, and gradually approximates towards a complete mental counterpart of it.

6. *The Space-Time Structure of Language*

And Space and Time in concord suited,
When Sounds to Symbols were transmuted.

This, then, is the unique characteristic of language that, while made out of the pure time expression of sound, it has by conventionalization been converted into an adequate space-time medium for translating a space-time world. By reverting to our illustration of the two circles representing the two worlds of nature and mind, one can make clear, by a well-selected example, the whole significant structure of language in relation to the actual world of space and time.

Let the picture in A represent an actual scene in the world of nature, then the language sentence in B will represent the same scene as translated by language into the corresponding world of mind. Here you have an actual complex space-time picture in the natural world transferred by language into the mental world, and set up there in a space-time synthesis in exact correspondence with the space-time synthesis in the natural world. The mental one is the counterpart of the natural one. Of the five connotative words three, "grey," "wolf," "field," are connotative of space, or objects of space, but "not marking time," as

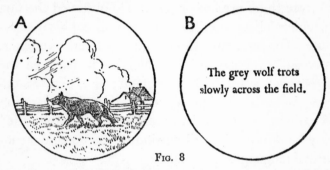

FIG. 8

Aristotle puts it (ἄνευ χρόνου, *Poetics,* xx. 8). Two of the three words, "wolf" and field," the nouns, are the primary classificatory names of objects in space, differentiating the genera (or species), as the scientist would say; the third word, "grey," the adjective, is a secondary or sub-classificatory word differentiating the species (or varieties) within the genus (or species).

The other two connotative words, "trots" and "slowly," connote time in the form of motion through space. Of these two words the first one, "trots," the verb, connotes the genus (or species) of motion, the second, "slowly," the species (or variety).

Furthermore, "trots" not only expresses time by connoting a species of motion, but by its inflected form it differentiates time as a *present* time. Aristotle's marking of this (*Poetics,* xx) is concise and to the point. "A verb is a composite significant sound, marking time. For 'man' or 'white' does not express the idea of 'when'; but 'walks' or 'has walked' does connote time, present or past." He observed the fact of which I have tried to give the philosophical exposition. The remaining significant word in the sentence, "across," expresses the spatial relation between the object and its spatial environment; also, to a less degree, a relation in time, since it carries the suggestion of motion. The weak demonstratives "the" and "the" may be omitted in a discussion of the general structure of language.

We have spoken above of the permanence of language in the world of mind in contrast to the transitoriness of the things of sense in the world of nature. To illustrate this distinction so as to complete the contrast, consider the same dual scene set out in Fig. 9 above, say five minutes afterwards, and we should find it as shown in the diagram on the following page. Here the central object of interest, the wolf, has disappeared from the sense picture of the natural world. The corresponding picture in the world of mind remains substantially as it was, with only the time word, "trots," altered by inflection to "trotted," to indicate that its original counterpart in the world of sense has disappeared, and belongs now to a past time and to things that have vanished.

This illustrates, as we have said, practically the whole structure of language, and, omitting for the time the abstract stratum of language as a later development which does not modify the original structure, then of the four connotative parts of speech,

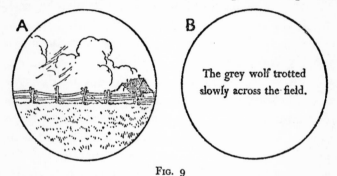

FIG. 9

two, the noun and the adjective, connote objects in space, the other two, the verb and the adverb, connote movements and sequence in time. The prepositions, originally prefixes or suffixes to connotative words, are the means of expressing relations of space, time, or cause. Conjunctions are used for synthesizing given parts into a more complex whole. The personal pronoun stands for the new individualized world of mind in man, the *ego,* as against the world of nature. That is virtually the whole structure of language which was from the beginning predetermined by the space-time structure of the worlds of nature and mind, and by the problem of translating the former into the latter, and setting it up there in a system corresponding to its own nature.

Language, however, is a conventional art; and while the problem confronting all nations and races of people is identical, each nation or race, working separately at it, would be bound to make its special language symbols and structure after its own fashion, so that the languages of the world are as various in their external features as are the peoples who made them. Nevertheless in two ways they are fundamentally the same; they are all made out of the raw material of sound, and they are all designed to translate a common world constructed in space and time. Suppose we take the natural scene of field and wolf given above, and turn it into several languages of different structures. We should then see clearly both the great variety in special features and the fundamental identity of language.

		1	2	3	4	5	6	7	8
English	(a)	The	grey	wolf	trots	slowly	across	the	field.
	(b)	The	grey	wolf	trotted	slowly	across	the	field.

		1	2	3	4	5	6	7	8
Greek	(a)	ὁ	γλαυκός	λυκὸς	τρέχει	βραδέως	διὰ	τοῦ	ἀγροῦ.
	(b)	ὁ	γλαυκός	λυκὸς	ἔδραμε	βραδέως	διὰ	τοῦ	ἀγροῦ.

		2	3	6	8	5	4
Latin	(a)	Ravus	lupus	trans	campum	lente	currit.
	(b)	Ravus	lupus	trans	campum	lente	cucurrit.

<pre>
               1   3   2   4   5   6   7   8
French (a) Le loup gris trotte lentement à travers le champ.
        (b) Le loup gris trotta lentement à travers le champ.

               1   2   3   4   5   6   7   8
German (a) Der graue Wolf lauft langsam durch den Feld.
        (b) Der graue Wolf lief langsam durch den Feld.

               1   2   3   5   4   6   7   8
Chinese (a)   此 白 狼   徐   跑 遏 此 田
        (b)   此 白 狼 巳 徐 跑 過 此 田
</pre>

(N.B.—I have numbered the corresponding words in the various languages to simplify the comparison.)

These are sufficient to illustrate the common substructure of language and the individual variations of languages. In 1830 the British and Foreign Bible Society published a pamphlet of 166 pages, in which a single well-known verse from the New Testament—"For God so loved the world that He gave His only begotten Son, that whosoever believeth in Him should not perish, but have everlasting life"—was rendered in 630 different languages and dialects. It was interesting to see the immense varieties in visual symbols and syntactic devices, and the common substratum of language structure, by which the same complex experience has been translated into the world of mind by various peoples.

It is true that in the abstract and complex development of language in the later reflective stages of its history, the fundamental space-time structure is often partially obscured by the fact that one connotative part of speech may be derived from another; but it is only obscured, never lost. When a noun, for example, is derived from a generic verb as in "running is strenuous exercise," the noun "running" still contains the time element of movement or change. This is true in all cases of derivation of one part of speech from another. The detailed consideration of these aspects of language belongs, however, to another place than the present treatise, to the science of language rather than the philosophy.

It should be noted also that while we have spoken here of mind as the space-time counterpart of nature with the task of building up within itself by the symbols of language a mental space-time structure corresponding to the physical space-time world which it intellects, that is not the whole story of language. The mind as a new cycle of world evolution, though determined in its basic structure by the cycle of objective nature below it, has characteristics of its own which by introspection it can analyze and elaborate and set out in language, so that the mind, the *ego,* when actualized in language is not only a reflex or counterpart of the world of nature, but also of itself. Psychology is concerned with this aspect. I have, however, confined myself to the first aspect of language in the present treatment for the sake of simplicity and clearness.

For similar reasons I have omitted any discussion

of the copula, though that is the element of language and grammar that constitutes the alpha and omega of logic. The copula is the instrument of definition by which the manifold elements which exist in implicit differentiation and synthesis in the natural world of sense are explicitly differentiated, reunited, and brought to the explicit synthesis of thought. But this multiform material upon which the copula is employed in definition is first of all gathered from the world of nature and arranged in the mind under the forms of space and time by means of concrete nouns and adjectives, transitive and intransitive verbs, adverbs, and prepositions. Given this primary material gathered and ordered from the world of sense, the mind then proceeds to analyse and resynthesize its elements by means of the copula in the various steps of logic, so that the copula may for the time being be omitted from the discussion of the primary structure of language. It will find its place in the detailed analysis of grammar when we come to the science of language in another volume.

To summarize, then, at this point. Man's problem was to intellect the world; to translate the types from the world of nature to the world of mind, and in this way elaborate the world of mind. It is the generation and evolution of a new world. This generation is a time process, and sound as a time expression was the direct and natural medium by means of which the generating process could be actualized. By articulation and conventionalization man succeeded in making sound express objects in space as well as sequence in time, and in this way transmuted sound into an adequate single vehicle for representing a space-time world.

CHAPTER X

LANGUAGE AND THE NATURAL ARTS OF SPACE AND TIME

"Behold at last the poet's sphere!
But who," I said, "suffices here?
For, ah! so much he has to do;
Be painter and musician too!

.   .   .   .   .

No painter yet hath such a way,
Nor no musician made, as they;
And gather'd on immortal knolls
Such lovely flowers for cheering souls.
Beethoven, Raphael, cannot reach
The charm which Homer, Shakespeare, teach."
ARNOLD, *Epilogue to Lessing's Laocoön.*

❖   ❖   ❖   ❖

NEVERTHELESS, THE SENSUOUS SOUND ELEMENT *does* remain as the substratum of articulate language, and as language issues from the lips it issues in the same time sequence as does pure sound, for example, in music. But here is the unique difference which separates language fundamentally from the other four arts. As language issues from the lips, the pure "time-ness" of it, as we might say, is immediately transmuted and absorbed in the conventionalized connotation which is arbitrarily given to the differentiated

sounds. Hence in the thought-process of intellecting
the world by language the actual space-time world is
translated first into pure time, that is, into sound, but
is immediately, in the very act as it were, retranslated
by the *conventionalization* of sound into its former
space-time structure within the world of mind.

This transformation of natural sound from a pure
time expression into a space-time expression, by conventionalization, which is the unique characteristic of
language as the instrument of conscious mind, has,
as I have said, been overlooked, so far as I know, in
the philosophical discussions of language. Lessing was
the first philosopher who classified and expounded
the arts upon the ground of the two forms of sense,
space and time. In his *Laocoön,* where he elaborates
the idea, he classified architecture, sculpture, and
painting as the space representative arts; music and
poetry as the time representatives. The *Laocoön* was
published in 1766, 170 years ago, and the classification worked out there has been generally accepted
since that time. Robert Louis Stevenson follows this
classification without substantial modification in his
essay on *Style in Literature,* 1885.

But the symbols of language in the dual function
which they perform are, as stated above, essentially
different from the media of the other arts. Architecture, sculpture, and painting all work in pure space
media of form or colour, and address their expressions to the sense of sight alone. Their representations

are strictly limited by the nature of space, and that in two ways. First, a picture or a statue is a fixed, immovable spatial image, representing only a single moment of time. It can have no movement, and hence cannot express time at all, although it may suggest time by the particular moment chosen, or by the symbolic arrangement of the parts of a complex picture, as, for example, Böcklin's "Vita Somnium Breve," a picture in three parts, childhood in the foreground, youth and romance in the middle ground, and old age and death in the background. But this is only a symbolic suggestion of the time process of life, not an actual representation of it.

Second, in proportion as it becomes great or unique as a work of art, the Parthenon, for example, or the "Sistine Madonna," or the "David" of Michelangelo, it cannot be duplicated, so that the individual piece of art remains an individual physical thing, and is limited to one particular place as any other physical object is. We have to travel to Athens or Dresden or Florence to see it. It cannot for this reason become an adequately expressive instrument of free mind, whose unique characteristic is its ubiquitous and omnipresent nature; it occupies space and time as its natural domain.

Music, on the other hand, working in natural sound, is a pure time expression without spatial dimensions, and is limited by the nature of time, also in two ways. First, as a pure time expression it addresses itself to the ear alone, and has no power of representing spatial objects that address themselves to the eye. Second, as a pure time expression it is evanescent. Uttered in one moment, it is gone in the next, as fleeting as time itself.

These four arts, then, all working in natural sensuous media, and addressing themselves directly to the sense organs of sight or hearing respectively, are each limited to the sense forms of either space or time. They are not the free symbols of representation, which the mind requires to elaborate its own biform world.

But with the symbols of language everything is different. The natural sound elements out of which it is made have been freed from their time limits by transmutation into conventionalized symbols. Furthermore, by conventionalization *these symbols have been transferred from the realm of the senses to the realm of the imagination.* This is a vital point in the problem. The fundamental difference between the senses and the imagination is that the senses as image faculties are restricted to their local environment in space and time. To make an impress on the senses the actual objects or sounds must be within the range of the sense organs of sight or hearing.

The imagination, on the other hand, as an image faculty, is freed from the sensuous space-time limits of the natural world; or in other words, the imagination is itself the supra-sensuous space-time world of free mind, the potential realm of all possible space-

time mental images, and the symbols of language
address themselves directly *through* the senses to this
inward world. The significant import of language
does not reside in the particular natural sound, shape,
colour, size, etc., of the particular set of spoken or
written words as they strike the ear or eye, as is the
case with the natural arts. The import resides in the
conventional meaning. Hence the mind must first
interpret the sound which strikes the ear—"horse,"
for example—and *then* the corresponding image rises
in the imagination, but not for the senses. If, for example, I quote here the words from Wordsworth,
suggested by the statue of Newton at Cambridge:

> Of Newton with his prism and silent face,
> The marble index of a mind for ever
> Voyaging through strange seas of thought, alone,

the actual form of the words that strike the eye—or
ear if orally quoted—has no natural resemblance
whatever to Newton, as had the marble statue. But
the conventional connotation of the words carried
through the sense organs of ear or eye to the imagination to which they are addressed, and not to the
senses, at once raises there the image of Newton and
the sleepless exploring activity of his mind. To see the
actual sculptured statue one must travel to Cambridge, where it stands in its particular niche in space.
But in the three lines of poetry, by translating the
image from the natural art of sculpture to the con-

ventional art of language, Wordsworth has transferred the likeness from the realm of sense to the realm of the imagination, and has thus liberated it from the rigid marble and its fixed point in space, and made it ubiquitous and omnipresent.

Furthermore, the marble gave us only the space representation of Newton, his physical appearance to the eye at one particular moment of his life. It gave us no time nor motion. The printed poetry, though presented to the eye in a fixed space-time pattern, gives us the time-movement of his mind as well, "for ever voyaging through strange seas of thought, alone." Wordsworth did not get this time-idea from the marble statue, but from his previous knowledge of Newton; though with this previous knowledge in his mind as he contemplated the statue in an unreflecting mental attitude, he might himself have imagined that he saw it in the marble. As pointed out above, the symbols of language, though originally made from the raw time-material of sound, are changed by conventionalization into a space-time medium so as to become the completely efficient instrument for the elaboration of the space-time world of free mind, whether presented to the mind through the ear in the time-forms of oral speech, or through the eye in the space-forms of written speech. In referring to written speech at this point, however, we are anticipating the matter of our next chapter.

CHAPTER XI

LAST STEP: TRANSLATION OF LANGUAGE FROM TIME TO SPACE

Words are fleeting in pronunciation, but permanent when written down.—BACON, *Advancement of Learning.*

Statues of brass or marble will perish; and statues made in imitation of them are not the same statues nor the same workmanship, any more than a copy of a picture is the same picture. But print and reprint a thought a thousand times over, and with material of any kind, carve it in wood or engrave it on stone, the thought is eternally and identically the same thought in every case. It has a capacity of unimpaired existence, unaffected by change of matter, and is essentially distinct and of a nature different from everything else that we know of or can conceive.—THOMAS PAINE, *The Age of Reason.*

⋄   ⋄   ⋄   ⋄

AND NOW WE COME TO THE FINAL STEP IN THE making of language. By the conventionalization of sound in oral speech, which is the actual language, man accomplished two things. First, he changed the vague suggestiveness of natural sounds into perfectly defined, articulated, limited sound symbols, that can be clearly differentiated from one another by the ear, as "rat," "cat." Second, by conventionalization he transformed the pure time symbols into space-time symbols, as in the sentence, "The bird sings," where "bird" is a representation of space, "sings" of time, though both are carried from the lips of the speaker to the ear of the listener upon the common substratum of sound, that is, time.

But this conventionalization of sound in oral speech did not completely solve the problem set to conscious reason, of raising above the transient world of nature a permanent and actual world of mind. Oral language even when conventionalized was still dependent upon the natural sound-element out of which it was made, and consequently was still under the limitations of time. It was evanescent; the pure flux of Heraclitus. As soon as the words were sounded they vanished, and at once ceased to exist, and when required again they had to be reproduced by the will and vocal organs, only to disappear immediately once more. There was no independent objective permanence at all in oral language. The only permanence was in the memory of the living individual that could produce the language again when required, and it had to be generated each time it was required. Without the presence of the living human agent the thing had completely vanished.

But the characteristic of the world of mind, as already noted, is that it combines permanency with

motion. As contrasted with the forward vanishing
series in the natural world, the world of mind advances by a cumulative movement, translating type
after type from the sensuous world of nature into its
own supra-sensuous world, and setting them up there
in a fixed non-vanishing structure. A man who writes
his diary, transferring the vanishing incidents of his
life in the natural world into the non-vanishing
medium (language) of the world of mind, would
illustrate the point, though we are going ahead of the
logic in illustrating it by written language at this
stage. Oral speech alone, because of its continually
vanishing nature, could not accomplish this. It could
not escape the evanescence of sound out of which it
is made. Consequently, in oral speech there was no
means of raising a fixed objective structure that
would preserve the vanishing time-sequence of things
and events in an ever-accumulating non-vanishing
present, as the nature of conscious developing reason
demands. In the activity of reason as we see it elaborating its own world to-day, in the written or printed
symbols of language, the significance of the natural
world is being steadily gleaned from its vanishing
stream, and being stored up in a non-vanishing continuously present world. The library of the British
Museum would illustrate adequately this cumulative
movement of reason, where the various phases
through which the world has passed in its previous
evolution, themselves now vanished in time, are pre-

served in a permanent present, a pure world of mind though stored in the sensuous material of paper and ink. If we think of what a university, say, would be without a single book, and without blackboards or notebooks, shut off from a vanished and irrecoverable past, we should have a picture of the limitations which time sets upon oral speech alone as an instrument of conscious mind.

To obtain the required permanence the time symbols of oral speech had to be converted in some way or other into space symbols, since space has that fixity which time lacks. Hence all nations that made any considerable advance in the elaboration of their mental world were led by instinct and necessity to search for some kind of space symbols, written speech as we now call it, that would crystallize and hold the vanishing stream of oral speech.

This, however, was a fundamentally difficult problem. Language is made out of sounds, and how could a sound be represented by a spatial picture? Or more explicitly, how could the fluent sound-symbols of actual oral language, which are expressed in time alone, and are without visual shape, be converted into non-fluent space-symbols, which would give them permanence without at the same time destroying the movement of time and thought? The difficulty of this problem is evidenced by the fact that there have been races of people who had developed a highly perfected oral language, reaching backward over many hundreds of years, who never succeeded in converting it into a corresponding written language. They were forced by this barrier to remain in a vanishing present world, isolated even from the most significant achievements in their own past history, so that they could make no appreciable progress at all in what we call civilization. The Cree Indians, for example, who lived for untold generations upon the plains of western Canada, had no written language prior to 1841, yet their oral language was as highly developed in its grammar and syntax as the English or any other modern civilized language. In 1841 the ingenious missionary, James Evans, invented for them a very simple system of syllabic writing into which parts of the Bible could be translated, and which is still extensively used among them.

The detailed account of the invention and perfecting of written language would be a long story if it could be fully told, and belongs to the science of language rather than to the philosophy. An attempt will be made to give what is known about it in a separate treatise on the Evolution of the Alphabet. Here it will be necessary only to suggest the main headings of the story.

The written speech in modern languages is merely an arbitrary and artificial spatial representation of the original language of oral speech. In the first steps of written language, however, there was no real connection at all between the written characters and the actual oral language. In every known case, so far as the records have come down to us, when man first felt the need of a written record to preserve a present experience for a future time, or to transmit it to someone at a distance from him in space, he began by pictorial representations of natural objects that were seen and known. A bird was represented not by "b-i-r-d," but by a picture of a bird, an animal by the picture of an animal, and so on. From these first natural drawings or pictographs man gradually moved forward to the next step, the ideograph, where the visual objects by symbolic associations were used in very crude ways to represent thoughts and actions and inner experiences. But this mode of written speech had still no connection at all with the real language of oral speech. Nor could it be called in any true sense a written language corresponding to oral language. It was at best but a lisping and fragmentary makeshift for language. It was merely a spatial representation of spatial things, and could give no organized synthesis at all of the space-time world which man was already organizing effectively in his oral speech.

Finally, and perhaps in all cases by some lucky combination of accident and ingenious thinking, the exact details of which are now lost in a long vanished and irrecoverable past, the momentous step was taken, when the ideographs became phonograms, that is, when the written characters became representations, not of things that are seen, but of sounds that are heard. How, precisely, this last step was taken, converting time into space, will perhaps never be fully known. In this way, however, the actual sound-symbols of oral language were translated into corresponding space-symbols, which preserves them from the evanescence of sound out of which oral language is made.

The conversion of the sound-symbols of time into corresponding form-symbols of space, which gave to language an accumulating permanence without destroying or altering its life and movement, was the consummation of the long language-making process. It was the most momentous and fruitful single achievement of the human intellect, since it was the condition of all the cumulative progress that man has since made in the world of free mind, which is his peculiar sphere.

In the development of the Aryan languages, the branch to which our own language belongs, this union of time and space symbols was accomplished in the evolution of the alphabet, where the oral sounds of language were resolved first into their twenty-six elements (I am again using arbitrarily the number in our own English alphabet) of vowels and consonants, and each one of these twenty-six attached to a separate space symbol, so that language became at one and the same time fluid and fixed; change and permanence united in a single synthesis. This actual union of motion and permanence is a new phenomenon in world evolution. The oral language is still the actual language, since it is the direct expression of the time movement of thought. The written language consists in the transference of this sound-language to a spatial representation, to preserve it from the evanescence of time. But in the transference, while the time movement is arrested and crystallized in space, it is not destroyed. The natural time sequence of the thought and the corresponding time-flow of oral speech are preserved first of all in the linear arrangement of the words on the spatial page. Second, the conventional connotation of the words themselves remains the same as in oral speech, by means of which, as we have already seen, language can express objects in space and sequence in time with equal facility.

The miracle—miracle, I mean, when compared with anything to be found in the world in the prelanguage stage of its history—that has been accomplished here can be clearly seen if we set out in written form three or four lines of poetry where movement and action—time expression—are the dominant quality. These from Burns's *Tam o 'Shanter,* for example:

> As Tammie glowered, amazed and curious,
> The mirth and fun grew fast and furious;
> The piper loud and louder blew,
> The dancers quick and quicker flew,
> They reeled, they set, they crossed, they cleekit,
> Till ilka carlin swat and reekit.

As soon as the vanishing oral expression is turned into writing, or print, it is arrested and becomes fixed and still; but the movement of the piper and the dancers continues. Though stilled in the spatial page the piper pipes on and the dancers dance. The actual dance ceased at midnight a hundred and fifty-odd years ago, vanished in time from the stage of the world. The representation of it in oral speech would have been as evanescent as time. But as soon as Burns turns it into ink, into visible symbols in space, the player plays and the dancers dance on for ever. Turned into print, the dance *movement* becomes, in Browning's phrase, an "eternal petrifaction." Or, in the abstract logic of prose, written language is the crystallization of the fluidity of time, while time still retains its movement and fluidity even while standing fixed and motionless in space. This, as it seems to me, is the unique characteristic of language which marks it off from all other phenomena of the world, the peculiar fusion of motion and permanence in a single synthesis without destroying the nature of either, and making language the completely adequate instrument of free and conscious mind.

CHAPTER XII

SUMMARY AND CONCLUSION

> The termination of the world in a man appears to be the last victory of the intelligence. . . . An individual man is a fruit which it cost all the foregoing ages to form and ripen. . . . Each individual soul is such, in virtue of its being a power to translate the world into some particular language of its own.—EMERSON, *The Method of Nature,* 1841.

> Our story of evolution ended with a stirring in the brain-organ of the latest of nature's experiments; but that stirring of consciousness transmutes the whole story and gives meaning to its symbolism.—EDDINGTON, *Science and the Unseen World,* 1929.

⋄   ⋄   ⋄   ⋄

1. *Deductions of Logic*

IT MAY BE WORTH WHILE NOW TO SUMMARIZE IN A page or two the view of world evolution as outlined above, a spiral structure of which man's created language forms the final story. In this summary I adopt the organic hypothesis, which assumes that mind is a basic and permanent element in the world, self-determining and purposive in its nature, and the directing agency in the evolutionary process throughout its history. While the acceptance or rejection of this

244

metaphysical hypothesis is not essential to the acceptance or rejection of the scientific exposition of the
birth and structure of language given in the preceding pages, the choice of one or other hypothesis does,
of course, make a rather complete difference in the
diction and phraseology chosen to set out the specific
exposition. To a mechanist many of the terms which
I have used may appear altogether unwarranted or
quite wrong. So far as that is true I ask his indulgence
for the use of those terms and turns of expression that
are dependent upon and consonant with the organic
hypothesis, and grant him the right to substitute his
own terms, where necessary, from the opposite hypothesis, but request only that he consider the specific
exposition of the birth and structure of language on
its own merits, without prejudice from the hypothesis
with which I have associated it. I accept the organic
hypothesis of a self-directing and purposive activity
in the world because it seems the only coherent and
logical view when one considers all the evidence from
matter to man. A self-directing and purposive activity
appears everywhere in the plant world, becomes more
pronounced and obvious in the animal world, and
emerges to explicit activity in man. Besides, the
whole series in the rising scale of world forms from
matter to man are causally related to one another in
the relation of sustaining and sustained. That the
upper part of the scale, the organic world, should
manifest explicit purposive and self-directing activity

in all its growth, life, and habits, seems more than mere presumptive evidence that the inorganic base out of which it arose and upon which it entirely depends for its life and all its purposive activities is also a purposive structure, though the purposiveness is not as yet apparent to human perception.

On this hypothesis, then, the life and mind of the world, which in its time-evolution rises steadily, and in an apparently unbroken ascending series, upward through the cycles of insentient and sentient life, eventually comes to a focus in the organism and mind of man, breaks through the enveloping forms of space and time, and emerges into free and conscious individualities. The world which was formerly a single sensuous world, in rising into this new cycle of its evolution, breaks, in a manner, into two worlds. The sensuous space-time world of nature is duplicated by the supra-sensuous space-time world of mind, which emerges now, radiating from individualized mind-points, and holds all space and all time in its single view; and turning back upon itself is confronted with the endlessly diversified forms of its own preconscious evolution. The task set then to the mind of the world, when it emerged to freedom and consciousness in the organism of man, was the task of entering into mental possession of the innumerable diversified forms of all the lower cycles of its own life-history. This it could do only step by step, by translating the multitudinous types of all its preconscious history one by one into its own supra-sensuous world of free mind. If there is any reality in the theory of the organic unity of the world and the natural evolution of its successive aspects in time, then man *is* the world at that point where it awakens to consciousness and turns back upon itself to explore and know its own nature; and this self-exploration, and the growing record of its results in language, constitute a new cycle in world evolution.

To accomplish this task of elaborating a new supra-sensuous world, patterned after the sensuous world of nature, man, with his newly emerged conscious mind, had to have for his new world-building material supra-sensuous symbols, freed, in some way or other, from the sense-limiting media of space and time. Specifically, he required time-symbols lifted above the evanescence of time, and space-symbols released from the fixity of space.

Starting with his own natural sounds, which as time-expressions were the natural symbols for the time-process of intellecting the world, but which in their natural state could express time-manifestations only, man first transmuted these natural sounds into definite and conventionalized sound-symbols, which could express manifestations of space as well as of time, and in this way made the adequate biform instrument for the translation of a biform world.

Next, to preserve this sound-language from the evanescence of time, man succeeded, after long experimentation, in translating his sound-symbols into corresponding space-symbols so as to secure permanence, without, however, destroying or altering the time-movement of oral speech. By this translation and consequent amalgamation of the symbols of time and space, so that the content could without alteration be expressed in either of these sense-forms, man gained for language that spaceless and timeless character which corresponds to the nature of free and conscious mind; motion and rest, change and permanency, fused in a single synthesis where each retains its own nature while freed from its own limits. The marriage of Heraclitus and Parmenides.

The other four arts, as pointed out above, each working only in space or in time, are only half-transmuted, as we might say, from nature to mind. They are only half-liberated from the sense limits of the natural world. Language by conventionalization and by amalgamation of the forms of time and space is freed from the limits of both; and in language, and in language alone, the mind has attained its full freedom, has created an efficient instrument for the elaboration of its new world. Hence all the intercourse of life is carried on in language as it alone expresses freely the double world of space and time in which man lives.

When Keats wrote his *Ode on a Grecian Urn* the rigid spatial beauty of the marble, arrested and motionless for centuries, was instantaneously liberated in the movement of time, even though it now stands still as marble again in the ink of the lines; motion and stillness in magic though actual combination. Keats was struck with the durability of the marble as contrasted with the vanishing beauty of natural life:

> For ever wilt thou love, and she be fair.

But to obtain this durability in marble all motion in time was excluded, a single moment given in fixed isolation from all before and after. Language restores the motion and life of time, and also invests the whole with a durability outlasting the marble's. By translating the beauty from the natural marble to the conventional symbols in ink, which may be mechanically reproduced and multiplied *ad infinitum* without loss of import, the beauty actually becomes a thousand times more durable than marble. A single accidental explosion could destroy the Parthenon. What accident, short of a world cataclysm, could destroy the *Odyssey,* multiplied and distributed as it is over the whole earth's surface?

2. *The Perception of Poetry*

We see then how far the monuments of wit and learning are more durable than the monuments of power, or of the hands. For have not the verses of Homer continued twenty-five hundred years, or more, without the loss of a syllable or letter; during which time infinite palaces, temples, castles, cities, have been decayed and demolished? It is not possible to have the true pictures or statues of Cyrus, Alexander, Caesar; no, nor of the kings or great personages of much later years; for the originals cannot last, and the copies cannot but lose of the life and truth. But the images of men's wits and knowledge remain in books, exempted from the wrong of time, and capable of perpetual renovation. Neither are they fitly to be called images, because they generate still, and cast their seeds in the minds of others, provoking and causing infinite actions and opinions in succeeding ages : so that, if the invention of the ship was thought so noble, which carrieth riches and commodities from place to place, and consociateth the most remote regions in participation of their fruits; how much more are letters to be magnified, which, as ships, pass through the vast seas of time, and make ages so distant to participate of the wisdom, illuminations, and inventions, the one of the other!—BACON, *Advancement of Learning.*

Since language attains its most precise and perfect expression in poetry it would not be unfitting to close a prose dissertation on language by some lines from poets who have thought and written about it. By a lucky chance the similarity and contrast between the natural arts and the conventional art of language can be clearly set out by setting side by side two sonnets by the two masters of their respective arts, and of thought as well, in their century, Michelangelo and Shakespeare. It so happened that Michelangelo died in the same year (1564) in which Shakespeare was born, a fact which gives an additional fortuitous interest to the comparison. Shakespeare was not a professional dialectician like Plato; at least, so far as we know, he did not practise the dialectic art. But he has a disconcerting habit of arriving at the last syllogism in a dialectical series without the labour of the intervening steps; so that when the logician has worked his slow way through a long dialectical process, and has arrived at the last syllogism which is to set out the consummating truth which he has been following, he unexpectedly meets Shakespeare at the end casually handing to him the same truth in a quite off-hand manner, as though he had incidentally picked it up by the wayside. I chanced upon his sonnet on Language in the dim recesses of memory after the foregoing treatise was completed.

Shakespeare was cognizant of the unique character of language in the world, and particularly of the power of arresting and preserving the vanishing things of the world of sense. Poets and philosophers had already reflected upon the durability of the natural plastic arts when contrasted with the fragile organic forms of nature; particularly sculpture, where the forms of beauty were "wrought in hard mountain marble." Of this time-resisting characteristic of the plastic arts Michelangelo has given us perhaps the most impressive image in his sonnet on *The Artist and his Work,* addressed to the beautiful and gifted Lady Vittoria Colonna, the friend of his later years. Part of the impress of his lines is due no doubt to the weight of evidence we feel behind them in Michelangelo's own works in sculpture.

How can that be, lady, which all men learn
By long experience? Shapes that seem alive
Wrought in hard mountain marble, will survive
Their maker, whom the years to dust return!
Thus to effect cause yields. Art hath her turn,
And triumphs over Nature. I, who strive
With sculpture, know this well; her wonders live
In spite of time and death, those tyrants stern.
So I can give long life to both of us
In either way, by colour or by stone,
Making the semblance of thy face and mine.
Centuries hence when both are buried, thus
Thy beauty and my sadness shall be shown,
And men shall say, "For her 'twas wise to pine." [1]

But even the "hard mountain marble," though in permanence far surpassing all natural forms of beauty, is not eternally immune from the effects of time. In the end it is only a matter of relative durability. Given a sufficient period of time, and time will change and wear down the marble also. This is what Shakespeare saw, that nothing in nature nor

[1] Cóm' esser, donna, può quel ch' alcun vede
Per lunga sperienza, che più dura
L'immagin viva in pietra alpestra e dura
Che 'l suo fattor, che gli anni in cener riede
La causa all' effetto incline e cede,
Onde dall' arte è vinta la natura.
Io 'l so, che 'l provo in la bella scultura;
Ch' all' opra il tempo e morte non tien fede.
Dunque posso ambo noi dar lunga vita
In qual sia modo, o di colore o sasso,
Di noi sembrando l' uno e l' altro volto:
Si che mill' anni dopo la partita
Quanto e voi bella fusti, e quant' io lasso
Si vegga, e com' amarvi io non fui stolto.

even in the plastic arts can eventually escape the never-ceasing detrition of time; that written language alone, because it is a conventional and not a natural art, addressing itself to the imagination, and not to the senses, and capable, therefore, of being illimitably reproduced without loss or modification of the substance of beauty which it transmits, written language alone has the unique power of transcending time and change, and of becoming thus the adequate instrument for elaborating that inward, supra-sensuous, non-vanishing world of mind in which man "lives and moves and has his being." Shakespeare perceived this clearly, and taking up the question where Michelangelo and the others had left it, he gave us in a single sonnet the most memorable statement that I know of this aspect of language, a statement where the lucidity of thought is made still more lucid by the "beauty imperishable" of the expression.

Since brass, nor stone, nor earth, nor boundless sea
But sad mortality o'ersways their power,
How with this rage shall beauty hold a plea,
Whose action is no stronger than a flower?
O, how shall summer's honey breath hold out
Against the wreckful siege of battering days,
When rocks impregnable are not so stout,
Nor gates of steel so strong, but Time decays?
O fearful meditation! Where, alack,
Shall Time's best jewel from Time's chest lie hid?
Or what strong hand can hold his swift foot back?

Or who his spoil of beauty can forbid?
O, none, unless this miracle have might,
That in black ink my love may still shine bright.

It would be hard to improve upon the clear logical image which Shakespeare has given us here of the unique character of language as a phenomenon among other phenomena of the world—its immunity from time and change, its silent and successful resistance to the "wreckful siege of battering days," to which all other forms in the world both of nature and of the natural arts must soon or late succumb.

THE END

INDEX